To the three pastors with whom I served and from whom I learned:

> *Dr. Louis Paul Lehman, prince of preachers*
> *Dr. Vance H. Webster, prince of pastors*
> *Dr. William F. Kerr, prince of theologians*

RESTORING BROKEN RELATIONSHIPS

DON BAKER

HARVEST HOUSE PUBLISHERS
Eugene, Oregon 97402

RESTORING BROKEN RELATIONSHIPS

Copyright © 1989 by Harvest House Publishers
Eugene, Oregon 97402

Library of Congress Cataloging-in-Publication Data

Baker, Don.
    Restoring broken relationships / Don Baker.
    ISBN 8-89081-722-7
    1. Interpersonal relations—Religious aspects—Christianity.
I. Title.
BC4509.5.B35   1989   89-35236
248.4—dc20   CIP

Contents

**Part III: How to Restore
Broken Relationships**

**Part IV: Togetherness in Meaningful
Relationships**

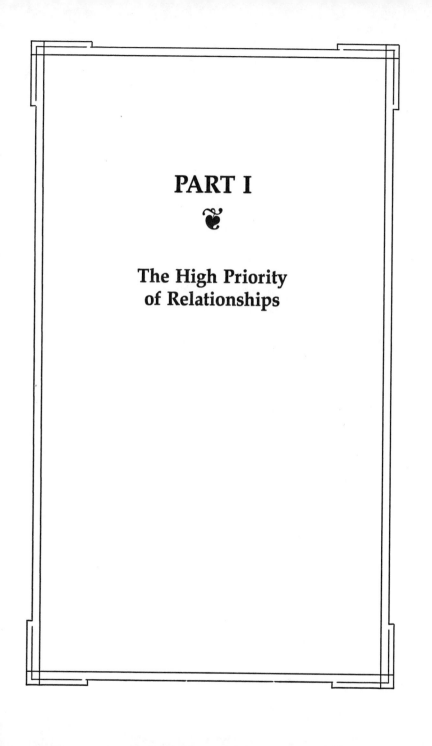

PART I

❧

The High Priority
of Relationships

1

Everybody Needs Somebody

❦

United's evening flight from Los Angeles to Portland was nearly full. I stowed my carry-on bag in the overhead bin, sat down in my assigned aisle seat, opened a new Robin Cook novel, and began to read.

I was tired. My brain needed to shut down, and my body wanted a rest. In the past 22 days I had traveled 23,000 miles and preached 35 times.

The two seats next to mine were empty. Is it just possible that I might have the luxury of three adjoining seats for the next 150 minutes I thought.

I watched the passengers as they shoved and squeezed their way through the first-class cabin, their eyes darting from their boarding passes to the seat numbers above the aisle. A controlled hostility began rising within me as each new stranger appeared.

I really wanted those seats.

The line finally thinned. The cabin attendants were instructed to prepare for departure. I breathed a sigh of relief, said, "Thank-you, Father," fluffed a couple of pillows, and moved toward the window.

Then I saw her.

The cabin door was reopened, and she was the last to board. She was out of breath, loaded with carry-ons, and destined to be my seat partner. As she squeezed past my seat, she gave me a big smile and a happy "Hi." I smiled limply in return.

She was young, attractive, and appeared to be disgustingly friendly. I really hoped she wasn't a talker. If I couldn't stretch out and sleep, at least I could enter into my own little personal oblivion for a while.

During the take off and meal service she made two attempts at conversation. My answers were polite but clipped and closed-ended.

Just as I leaned my seat back and closed my eyes, she reached into her bag and pulled out a paperback and a ball-point pen. As she read, I noticed that she was also underlining what must have been some very important thoughts.

Now those of us who write have an insatiable curiosity about humanity's reading habits—especially when humanity begins underlining what it reads. If anyone has said anything in print worth drawing a line under, I want to know what it is, and how it was said.

Out of the corner of half-closed eyes I caught the title. It was *Beyond the Barriers* by Harold Morris. I knew the book, its story, and a little about the author.

This quiet one came out of his self-imposed obscurity and became the talker. I leaned over, pointed to the book cover, and said, "That's a good book you're reading."

"Oh, have you read this book?" she asked.

"No, but I've scanned it and read some very positive reviews about it."

She began excitedly telling me about its content and added, "It's one of the best books I've ever read."

I wondered if she'd ever read one of mine.

I asked her name. It was Julie.

"Hi, Julie," I said. "I'm Don Baker."

"Don Baker? Don Baker? I think I've heard that name somewhere."

"I've written a few books, too," I said.

I named a dozen titles before suggesting one for which she had a vague recollection. As she was trying to recall its contents, I was convinced that if she had ever read the book, she certainly hadn't found anything worth underlining.

Julie was single, a Young Life staff member, and the creative director for an advertising firm. She had graduated from a Christian college in eastern Washington.

I asked, "Where do you attend church, Julie?"

She blushed, lowered her eyes, and said, "I'm really embarrassed to tell you. Actually I go to four churches."

"Four churches?" I asked.

"Yes, four churches. And I go to all four of them regularly."

"Which four?"

"Well," she said. "I go to the Presbyterian church, the Foursquare church, the Catholic church, and the Baptist church."

"What are you looking for—the truth?"

"No, I know the truth. What I'm looking for is a church home."

"Don't any of those meet your requirements?"

"No," she said, "but all of them together almost meet my needs."

"Why have you picked those particular churches, Julie?"

"My roots are in the Presbyterian church. I've attended there most of my life, I'm comfortable with their liturgy, I know the pastor and he knows me, my friends are there, it's my parents' church, and it's where I was baptized."

"Well then you're a Presbyterian," I said.

"Yes," she said. "I guess I'm a Presbyterian, but, then again, I'm not a Presbyterian. Only part of me is satisfied when I leave the services on Sunday morning. Actually, I often leave feeling quite empty. I'm familiar with things as they are, but my friends there are really not much closer to me than my college friends or my friends outside the church."

"What about the Foursquare church?" I asked.

"I love the Foursquare church. They're so alive and expectant. They're friendly. I love the way they sing—and they sing a lot. The songs are fresh and new and different. We seldom sing from the hymn books, and I like that. The pastor doesn't know me, but he's warm and relational and usually says something that I can think about through the week. I'm uneasy with some of their doctrine and a little uncomfortable when they raise their hands, but I can handle that."

"Do you prefer the Foursquare church to the Presbyterian church?"

"In some ways, but not enough to leave my family church."

"What about the Catholic church? I can't think of any church less like the Foursquare church than the Catholic church, and yet you attend both."

"I like the Catholic church, too. It speaks with authority. It has a sense of history. It has dignity. It has form. It has tradition. Everything's predictable. There are no surprises. I don't know anybody there, but I don't go there to meet people. I go there to meet God. I don't always understand what they're doing, but then I don't feel I have to, since I've just gone there to worship."

"What about the Baptists?"

"Baptists know their Bible, and they seem to have a sense of mission. They want people to know Christ, and I believe in that. Sometimes they're too informal for me, and sometimes they act like they're the only ones who have the truth, and I don't like that, but they seem to love me, and pray for me, and encourage me."

"Julie, where do you sense the presence of Christ the most?" I asked.

She thought for a moment and then said, "In the Foursquare church, I think."

"Where do you have the most friends?"

"In the Presbyterian church."

"Where do you feel you get your best teaching?"

"I think that would be the Baptist church."

"Where do you have your most satisfying experience of worship?"

"In the Catholic church."

"If you had to choose one above all the rest, which one would it be?"

"Oh, I couldn't make that choice, not now anyway. Young Life is satisfying most of my needs. Not all of them—but most of them."

I had forgotten my tiredness. She'd forgotten her book. We talked until the wheels of Flight 1222 touched down on the runway at Portland's International Airport.

I asked her, "What is it you're really looking for, Julie?"

"What am I looking for?" She searched thoughtfully for an answer as she tucked her book back into her flight bag. She gathered up the rest of her belongings, placed them in the seat between us, and said, "I guess I'm looking for one church that meets all my needs—

"I want the Scriptures taught so I can understand them—

"I want truth made portable so that I can live it—
"But I want more—I want a church
  • where people are bonded together

- where they love each other as much as they claim to love Christ
- where people care for each other and share with each other
- where people are learning how to communicate honestly with each other
- where relationships go deeper than the masks of our composure
- where people are committed to each other
- where I'm free to fail, and
    free to succeed, and
      free to weep, and
        free to rejoice, and
          free to be different.

I do want truth, and
  I do want holiness, and
    I do want meaning for my life.

"But, I guess I'm looking for a church where relationships are as important as theology, and people more important than programs.

"I guess I'm just looking for meaningful relationships. I expected to find them in a church, and I guess I'm frustrated and disappointed that I haven't."

I wanted to question her further, but the 727 had rolled up to the gate, opened its door, and Julie, along with the others, moved quickly up the jetway and was gone.

We Weren't Meant to Go It Alone

I'm seldom unhappy when one of my long flights comes to an end. On the flight from Los Angeles to Portland I could have wished for a little more time.

I wanted to further explore Julie's thoughts on relationships. I wanted to probe for the meaning of some of the powerful words she used. I wanted time to respond to her longing for meaningful relationships with some observations of my own.

I wanted to tell her that Christians are the only people in the world who are capable of experiencing meaningful relationships.

I had also wanted to tell her how flattering it is to the old when the young are willing to share their concerns and their dreams.

What I wanted especially to say was that our longings and dreams were really quite similar. When one speaks of a search for meaningful relationships, he's actually addressing humanity's greatest hunger.

God spoke of that longing in Genesis as He prepared to create a companion for his first human. He said,

> It is not good for the man to be alone . . .
> (Genesis 2:18).

Loneliness has stricken nearly 50 million Americans with what some call a nationwide epidemic.

It's characterized by a feeling of isolation, of standing apart from others. It's a feeling of emptiness and a craving for companionship.

John Gunther refers to it as one of the supreme American problems.

Loneliness can have a profound effect on physical health. James J. Lynch, professor of psychology at the University of Maryland School of Medicine, was asked how close is the connection between loneliness and physical health. He said:

> That's like asking what is the connection between air and one's health. Like the air we breathe, human companionship is taken for granted until we are deprived of it. The fact is that social isolation, sudden loss of love and chronic loneliness

> are significant contributors to illness and
> premature death. Loneliness is not only
> pushing our culture to the breaking point,
> it is pushing our physical health to the
> breaking point.[1]

Age means very little when we begin to address the frightening presence of loneliness in our lives. We're born with an instinctive craving for meaningful relationships.

During the Korean War so many orphaned babies were born that hospital cribs and beds were no longer available. Staff nurses began substituting wooden boxes that looked like our present-day apple boxes.

Newborn babies were placed side by side in rows of boxes that had been softly cushioned with pillows and blankets. The babies were comfortable. They were clean, and they were cared for just like the others.

But they began dying. The infant mortality rate rose alarmingly.

Hospital staff members began checking for infections, tainted food supplies, foul air, improper handling—anything that might explain the sudden rise in the death rate.

A psychiatrist was called in. After lengthy observation he said, "I think they're lonely."

"They're what?" exclaimed an exasperated doctor.

"They're lonely," was the quiet response. "They can't see each other. The sides of the boxes are too high. Even newborns need to feel the presence of others. When they can't see any signs of life around them, their little spirits will shrivel and they'll die."

The sides of the boxes were cut down just enough for small eyes to catch the movements of life nearby. The death rate dropped back to normal. They were lonely.

Loneliness for a Lifetime

I don't know if that hunger for meaningful relationships is ever completely satisfied, but I do know that it lasts for a lifetime.

My 91-year-old mother is lonely. She's been widowed now for nearly 40 years. To fill the empty hours, she went to work as a college housemother. She mothered collegians, both men and women, for more than 20 years—nearly 500 of them.

They kept her young.
  They kept her awake.
    They gave her "fits" at times, but
      they also gave her a reason for living.
      But she was still lonely.

She wanted more than just "hellos" and "goodbyes" from the students, and so she would pop corn in her little apartment. She would then open her door so that the irresistible fragrance of popping corn would find its way to the upper floors and eventually entice some of her young friends to her room so that she wouldn't have to watch television by herself.

Every afternoon she would board a city bus, get off at one of the large shopping malls, and just stroll through the shops.

Why?

"That's the loneliest time of my day," she would tell us. "When you were young, that was the time of day when you children would begin arriving home from school.

"I'd have milk and cookies ready. You'd tell me about your day. The silent piano would come to life, or the radio would turn on. Preparation for supper would begin.

"That was when life began again at our house. I just can't stand to be alone in the afternoons."

When she was no longer able to work in the schools, she became a foster grandparent. At 90, she was still riding a city bus each day, just for the privilege of holding a child, hearing its laughter, or wiping away its tears.

Today she's alone—very much alone—confined to a nursing home, in a strange bed, with a roommate who can't speak, nurses who are too rushed, and a family that's always too busy.

She lives for our visits. Her face lights up when we walk through the door. Her body relaxes when we kiss her. Her little world comes alive with just two words, "Hi, Mom."

But then when we leave, she lapses back into her isolation, and we continue struggling with the guilt that rebukes us for not giving her more of ourselves and more of our time.

I have tended the sick and the dying all my life, but now that my own mother is confined and slowly slipping away from us, I feel so incompetent and clumsy. I sometimes wonder who is the most lonely— the dying or the living.

Generations of Loneliness

Everyone's lonely.

Everyone wants a meaningful relationship with someone.

Children want meaningful relationships.

We were enjoying a springtime supper on the back deck with part of our family when I noticed our two-year-old granddaughter climb down from her high chair, back away from the table, and then lapse into silence. There was a slight hint of a tear in her eye.

Her father had just finished building a beautiful play area adjacent to the deck, with swings and slides and a trapeze bar. At one end was every child's dream— her own sandbox.

We noticed her silence, and she was urged to go play. She didn't move.

I called her to me and then whispered, "Would you like grandpa to play in your sandbox with you?"

She came to life, took my hand, and we bounded down the steps, climbed into the sandbox together, and spent an ecstatic hour filling and emptying her little red sand bucket.

Not even swing sets and sandboxes can replace the touch of another human in a child's life.

Young people want meaningful relationships.

Mark lived in a half way house near one of the churches I pastored. His dress was always a little bizarre, consisting of a coonskin cap, dark glasses, a camouflage jacket, fatigue trousers, and paratroop boots.

He always arrived for church late and then walked across the auditorium to take a seat right in front of the pulpit.

Whenever I gave an invitation for people to come forward to receive Christ or to unite with the church, he would always be the first. No matter how many times we would remind him that it was unnecessary to keep coming forward, he would continue to come. One day he finally told me why. His reason: "I know you love me, Pastor Baker, and I just want to come down to stand beside you."

Those are the words that loneliness speaks.

Marriage is God's provision for humanity's loneliness, and yet many married couples live in the same house but are isolated emotionally. Jack H. Medalie and Uri Goldbourt made a recent study of 10,000 married men who were 40 years or older. The study was designed to determine factors contributing to angina pectoris, a type of heart disease. Men were studied over a five-year period. The study revealed that fewer of those who had loving and supportive wives developed angina pectoris than did those whose wives were nonsupportive (52 per thousand versus 93 per thousand).[2]

Marriages begin with a couple's mutual craving for a meaningful relationship and often end without either person ever experiencing it.

One of the world's wealthiest women, Christina Onassis, said just before she died, "I'd give all I own for a relationship with just one person who would love me for who I am rather than for what I own."[3]

I called a dear friend recently. We've known each other for more than 40 years. We dubbed each other with nicknames when we were young. They've stuck. I'm Peck-a-loomer and he's Frick-a-frack.

He and his wife are just one year away from celebrating their fiftieth wedding anniversary. He's been active in the business community and in churches all his life. He's well known, highly respected, and well liked.

I asked him, "How many close friends, besides your wife, can you count at this time in your life?"

"Oh, that's easy," he replied, "just one."

"Who," I asked.

"You."

I was honored. I was also saddened. As one ages, it soon becomes obvious that a person's true wealth is not counted in dollars, but in friends.

I'm lonely.

Martha's lonely.

We've spent a lifetime with people—thousands of them. Most of our relationships have been professional rather than personal. Those thousands of people assume today that we're either too busy or too overwhelmed with acquaintances to make room for them. The result is that we're lonely.

The measure of loneliness is not determined by the number of relationships one has established, but by the depths of those relationships.

We've lived in our little community for nearly two years now, and still no one in our supermarket can call us by name.

Recently I noticed that they had installed a Successful Living bookrack and that one of my books, *Lord, I've Got a Problem*, was there.

I purchased one—at the full price—took it over to the book counter, asked the cashier her name, inscribed the words—"Thank-you for selling my books, Jill," and then autographed it.

She was ecstatic. She said she'd never met an author before. She would read it—tonight. She would tell everyone about it.

When I walked away, she said, "Don Baker, you've made my day."

I thanked her. The thing that she didn't know was that she'd just made my day. It wasn't her comments about the book or her delight at meeting an author.

My joy was that finally somebody knew my name.

I would like to have said to my seat companion on Flight 1222, "I guess that's where we all are, Julie. You're looking for the same thing I'm looking for—everyone's looking for—to be known and accepted and loved in a way that satisfies that hunger for a meaningful relationship."

2

Potholes on the Road to Relationships

❦

I would also have said to Julie, "I'm not surprised that you've begun your search for a meaningful relationship in a church—in fact, I'm pleased.

"I wish you success.

"But to be perfectly candid with you, I'm not sure that you're going to find what your looking for in many of today's organized churches."

When Julie speaks of finding a church where

relationships are as important as theology, and where

people are more important than programs, and where

oneness is the norm,

I'm not certain that many Christians know what she means or even want to find out.

Some will think she's radical.

Others will call her heretical while still others will look upon her dream as being unattainable, or too threatening to even seek after.

I agree with Julie, that the church is the place where we should find people who

care, and
share, and

    love, and
     accept, and
     communicate, and
      commit themselves to one another.
The church was designed to be a place where
  we are free to fail,
   free to succeed,
    free to weep,
     free to rejoice, and
      free to be different.

Jesus' original intention for His church was that it was to be a place where loneliness was to be banished forever.

Our Lord died not only to bring us together with God, but also to bring us together with each other.

Many of us have placed most of our emphasis on helping people to know and love God, and we've failed to address the emptiness that comes from not knowing how to know and love one another.

I was reminded of this failure one Monday morning as I drove up to my reserved slot in the church parking lot.

The owner of an apartment house across the street came screaming through her front door, saw me, and told me to come quickly.

When I reached her, her entire body was trembling. She dissolved in my arms and tried to tell me something I couldn't understand.

She finally motioned for me to come.

I followed her up the front steps, in the door, and down a long, unlighted hallway. She opened an apartment door and motioned me inside.

It took a few moments to adjust to the poorly lit room. The shades were drawn. The television was blaring its meaningless message, and then I saw her.

She was hanging from the end of a rope that had been slung over one of the living room beams. Her neck and face were contorted in a hideous fashion. Her lifeless eyes stared down at me and seemed to follow every movement I made.

I slowly backed out of the private little death chamber, tried desperately to control the shaking of my own body, and then called the police.

I helped the officers gently lower her body and cover it with a blanket. It was only then that I could divert my eyes from that young woman.

Everywhere I looked in that little room, I saw evidences of loneliness.

The television was still on.

An empty box of See's chocolates sat in the middle of the coffee table.

A half-empty bottle of diet Coke was on the floor.

Empty glasses were everywhere.

Crumpled cigarette packs and stubs littered the area where she had sat.

—All kinds of pills—

The liturgy of death, I thought.

Mute evidences of loneliness.

I was curious.

I asked the landlady if this woman had ever visited the church.

"Yes," she said. "Only yesterday. She had just moved in last week and had been here long enough to tell me about all the sorrows in her brief lifetime. She had separated from her husband, been rejected by her parents, lost her job, and had claimed to have no friends whatever. I asked her to go to church with me Sunday.

"She did. We walked across the street in silence, sat together during the service, and on the way back to the apartment I asked her how she liked it.

"She was silent a long time. It was not until she had slipped through the door to her room that she looked at me and said, 'No one even said, "Hello." '

"She then closed her door quietly, and that was the last I saw of her until this morning."

Priorities Out of Alignment

A major part of the well-balanced diet of Christianity has been neglected. Something is missing in the sanctuary. The organized church has failed to see and hear the cries of the lonely. The human soul suffering from the pain of alienation is expressing its gnawing hunger for meaningful relationships—not only with God but with fellow humans.

A pastor said to me recently, "Well, I think I have finally got my priorities straight."

"What are they?" I asked.

"Evangelism, discipleship, and worship," he answered.

"Where are relationships?" I asked.

"Oh, they're in there, but just not all that important."

As I review my 40 years of ministry, I marvel at my own struggle with biblical priorities.

When I started out, I didn't have any. I didn't know there were any. I was swinging my biblical club at the writhing tail of liberalism; I was

sharing Christ with the lost,
preaching the Word,
visiting the sick,
marrying the young,
burying the dead,

but most of my time was spent trying to keep church bills paid and church members reasonably happy with me and with each other.

I developed a small degree of cynicism about my role which finally surfaced one day when somebody asked, "How are things going?" My answer was, "I'm keeping the lawn mowed."

Maintenance seemed to be the priority. If we could just keep the doors open, the people coming, our missionaries on the field, and increase our budget by an incredible two to three percent per year, then we were doing the job.

But other priorities slowly began coming into focus.

World War II provided a global vision for millions of GIs. The church began cranking up its enthusiasm for missions and nearly 40,000 of us went to foreign lands to preach Christ. Foreign missions became our priority.

Southern Baptists exalted Sunday School growth to a level of great importance in the early 1950s. The Sunday School became a priority.

New church buildings and the relocation of churches from urban to burgeoning suburban plots captured our attention in the '60s. As the nation's economy grew, the church became fiscally ambitious and erected its magnificent and expensive structures. But people were still lonely.

The Jesus Movement of the '60s focused the church's attention on a generation of druggies and flower children. We looked wide-eyed at photos showing long-haired, sandal-wearing hippies sitting cross-legged in the aisles of churches like Calvary Chapel. We yearned to rescue the unwitting victims of pot, acid, and rock music from the brink of destruction.

Dr. George Peters of Dallas Theological Seminary and Dr. Bill Bright of Campus Crusade for Christ began calling us back to the priority of evangelism in the late '60s. I remember being exposed to both and coming away from conferences on evangelism reveling in the simple challenge to outreach that seemed like a brand new truth. Protestants and Catholics alike began stressing evangelism.

The birth of new believers required instruction and nurture. A new thrust in discipleship emerged. Howard Ball and his "Churches Alive" staff provided invaluable help in simplifying the process of training church leadership. I had always resisted discipleship in my ministry. Not because of any biblical or theological argument—but because of my own personal insecurity. It was so much easier to teach than to train. Training required observation and practical experience. To tell was always easier than to show.

Along with nurture came the need for understanding about the gifts of the Spirit. Dr. Earl Radmacher of Western Conservative Baptist Seminary reopened the eyes of the church to the spiritual gifts distributed among the saints. But people were still lonely.

Church growth emerged in the '70s and '80s as priority number one. Statistical evaluations and appraisals of growing churches and mission ministries filled books and flooded the market. We were all tempted to tell our stories.

The challenging emphasis on growth was exciting for those churches that grew. It was baffling and terribly discouraging to those that didn't.

Dr. Ron Allen rediscovered the missing jewel of worship in the '80s, and new and various forms of worship were devised. Contemporary praise choruses crept into our services—and also provided us with a new struggle. Many of our older members didn't like them. Many left the churches where they were being used. But worship became our priority. People were still lonely.

The world began exposing hypocrisy in the church during the '80s. Names like Jim Bakker and Jimmy Swaggart captured the national headlines. Purity became the watchword, and church discipline was elevated to a place of practical prominence. We learned the meaning of the word "restore" and used it to replace the inadequate and destructive word "punish."

During these past four decades, evangelicalism, fundamentalism, and mainline congregations were still reeling from the great doctrinal disputes of the '20s and '30s. Many denominations and associations were born out of dispute. Many contended for the faith until they eventually became contentious. We fought so much and so long, that words like "unity" and "oneness" and "love" and "caring and sharing" became suspect.

The problem has not been limited only to the organized church.

The Julies of this world have grown up in a narcissistic society. People are primarily interested in themselves.

The "Yuppie" mentality has obsessed the young with an upward mobility craze that demands wealth and fame, no matter what the cost.

The "me generation" has placed utmost importance on

> what *I* want,
> what *I* think,
> what *I* do,
> what *I* don't do,

and has given very little concern and attention to others.

The "self-esteem gospel" has caused all of us to become introspective and self-seeking—again to the exclusion of others.

People are more transient,
  too busy,
    more mobile.
      We lack roots,
        and we lack the time

it takes to build a quality relationship with another person.

In this age of instant everything, it's awfully hard to accept the fact that a meaningful relationship takes time—lots of it.

God designed us for meaningful relationships, so I'm not surprised that Julie hungers for that kind of relationship, and I'm not surprised that she's seeking to find it in a church.

It's sad, tragically sad, that what we all crave can't even be found where that craving was designed to be satisfied—in the church.

I think that some of my strongest feelings of loneliness have been felt in a church. Maybe my expectations were too high or it may be that I'm the one who didn't allow others to minister to that need, but I, the pastor, have often been lonely in a church.

Years ago I visited one of the nation's great evangelical churches. It's well known for its size, its location, its history, and its strict adherence to truth.

I was alone.

It was terribly cold.

I knew no one.

I had walked for blocks in bone-chilling weather to get there, and when I finally arrived, it seemed as cold on the inside as it had been on the outside.

People sat next to one another like sticks on a pew.

Every movement seemed mechanical and contrived.

The greetings—and there were only a few—seemed hollow and meaningless.

No instruction was given about what to sing or when. We were all supposed to know that.

I stood once when I should have remained seated and felt the stinging embarrassment of disapproving stares.

When the visitors were asked to stand, I remained seated—I had already done that.

The sermon was correct and biblical. It was communicated well, but it seemed impersonal and irrelevant. It didn't touch me where I hurt that morning.

After the service people turned to their friends with the meaningless chatter that had no bearing whatever on what had just been said or felt.

No one greeted me, even though I waited and waited.

As I walked out of the building into that sub-zero day, I looked vainly for a taxi or a bus. A car drove up to the curb and stopped. The driver jumped out and said, "Here I am, climb in."

He opened the back door for me, and in that moment my whole world came to life. My loneliness was forgotten in the presence of an unexpected kindness.

My new friend climbed behind the steering wheel, started the car, and then turned to look at me. His expression changed as he suddenly realized that he'd picked up a stranger.

"Oh," he said, "you're not our guest speaker. I'm supposed to take him to his hotel. You'll have to get out."

I got out.

I trudged back to my little room at the Y.M.C.A. and I wondered—is this the way strangers feel when they come to our churches?

In my present role as a minister-at-large, I'm in a different church each week. In most of these churches I'm a stranger. No one knows me unless they've studied my picture carefully and then they're not always sure.

I like to stand in the halls or in the foyer or even sit alone in a seat and then wait to see what happens.

I walked into a church auditorium early one Sunday morning. It was empty except for the soloist and the sound man who was playing her taped accompaniment and regulating the volume.

I listened until the man turned and said, "I'm sorry sir, but you'll have to leave the auditorium until we're finished rehearsing."

I left.

In another church I stood and watched the choir members as they hurried to rehearsal, the ushers as they were given their last-minute instructions, the pastor as he checked the pulpit and his microphone.

I listened as the organist perfected her prelude and as the pianist searched for an elusive note she had been unable to find.

I watched as the children came into the building, excitedly screaming their greetings to one another.

I studied each adult face as it strained to find its destination and each family as it hurried to meet its deadline.

I searched for just one pair of eyes that would see me. It wasn't important that they should recognize me—I just wanted them to see me.

Just a little smile—or even a slight hint of awareness. A warm, friendly "Hi" would have helped. But there was none.

I noticed a man seated by himself, busily studying his copy of the Sunday bulletin. I decided that it was now time to find someone—anyone who would talk with me.

Walking over to where he was seated, I said, "Hi, what's your name?"

A noticeable frown creased his brow as he reluctantly looked up from his reading. "What do you mean, what's my name?" he asked. "What's yours?"

"I'm Don Baker," I said as I reached out to shake his hand.

"Oh," he said, hardly changing his expression, "I didn't think you were coming until next Sunday."

I've stood as a stranger in the line of greeters, waiting to shake the hand of the pastor. I've felt the limp, quick shake and the left hand that grabbed my elbow to hasten me along. I've looked into the eyes that didn't see me and heard the words that were intended for no one in particular.

I've been greeted by "greeters" who are doing their job, I've been held back at the door by ushers who reminded me that I was late, and I've been seated by those who walked me down the aisle, directed me to my seat, and handed me a bulletin without ever once seeing me.

I've tolerated the scowls of those who are forced to stand, shift their feet, or move their bodies to allow me to sit down.

But only as a stranger.

Things are so different when they know that I'm the visiting speaker. They just can't do enough to make me comfortable.

Not all churches are that way, I'm sure. But it's sad that any church should allow people to ever become that unimportant.

So, I'm pleased that Julie is looking for meaningful relationships in a church. That's where they're supposed to be found. But I fear that she may have to continue attending four churches to have that need plus all her others completely satisfied.

I'm trying to help churches see that this is humanity's great cry today—to see that relationships should reach priority status.

I'm trying to tell them.

It's time now—time to add a new priority—one that's as old as the Gospel.

It's time to recognize humanity's loneliness.

It's time to stop fighting and start loving.

It's time to stress relationships.

It's time to preach unity.

It's time to emphasize oneness.

It's time to lift Christians out of their isolation and alienation and elevate them to their place of original intention.

It's time for the world in its loneliness to catch a glimpse of Christians at peace.

It's time for a satisfying oneness to emerge as the sharp evangelistic tool that every believer can employ.

It's time for the Body of Christ to become so irresistibly attractive to the world that hostile, alienated people will seek it out as the solution to their loneliness.

It's time for Christians to give the same high priority to relationships that Christ did.

3

Is There Anything More Important than Worship?

❦

Worship is the "in" thing today. It's projected as the ultimate act of Christianity. It's esteemed, revered, and elevated in our lives. The Christian world is absorbed with thoughts of worship. Nothing takes precedence over worship, we think. But we're wrong. Relationships do. And reconciliation does when relationships have been broken.

Jesus stated that worship must be interrupted if relationships are not secure. "Leave your offering there before the altar," He said. Don't leave your mate, your family, your friend, your job, your parents, even your church as many of us do when fractures occur. "Leave your offering . . . and first be reconciled to your brother." Jesus, who is the object of our worship, admonishes us to interrupt our worship of God in order to secure our relationships with man. Why?

Relationship Above Worship

Broken relationships are distracting. Let's suppose you're walking through your favorite mall when you suddenly spot a close friend. You smile, wave, and then walk toward her with a warm greeting. But her greeting is less than warm. Her usual friendly eyes are cold. The smile is feigned and forced. What do you do?

If you're like me you probably don't say anything. You just walk away and worry a lot. You think, *I wonder what's wrong with her. What did I say that I shouldn't have said? What did I do that I shouldn't have done? What didn't I say? What didn't I do?* Your thoughts are flooded with disturbing, unanswered questions about a relationship which has mysteriously gone sour.

Furthermore, your personal prayer and study time is disrupted by memories of a disrupted relationship. In your valued time of personal worship you sing, pray, praise, read, and listen—but with distraction. Every significant upward thought is blurred by a disturbing sideward memory. Worship of God is diminished by the thoughts of a problem with a friend.

Jesus says, "Stop the pretense. Stop the attempts at worship. Go and repair the fractured relationship with reconciliation."

Worship is too important to be diluted by distractions. Worship demands our full attention.

Broken relationships are destructive. When a stranger enters your church, his first impression is purely subjective. His sensors are extended and he's feeling for impressions and expressions of warmth and peace and love and concern. He's searching for signs that he'll be accepted. He's probably not greatly interested in theology. And if he's not a Christian he's probably not even interested in salvation. Most likely he doesn't even realize that he needs it. He's interested in acceptance.

He immediately detects the difference between the church greeter who is assigned the task of being friendly and the member who is sincerely interested in him as a person. He feels rejection if he's forced to find his seat by himself. He gets angry if he's required to climb over the outstretched feet of those already seated. He sees the sidelong glances of those whose space he has intruded.

The visitor looks for signs that he's been expected. But instead he's embarrassed by a ritual or liturgy that fails to consider the fact that he doesn't quite know how to do it. He's humiliated when he's asked to take a Bible he doesn't have and look up a reference he could never find. He feels left out when he's called upon to join in singing a song he doesn't know.

He's especially aware of disharmony between people. He senses hostility in the congregation—if it's there—in the same way we feel it when we walk into someone's home after a family feud. Fractured relationships can be felt. Harmony and peace create an electricity of expectancy and excitement, and the stranger comes looking for it. If it's not there he doesn't return. The relationship gap between the stranger and the congregation, and the relationship gaps between the worshipers themselves, can turn a seeker away unfulfilled.

I was sitting on the platform one Sunday waiting for the service to begin. As I always do, I was looking out over the congregation, holding little unspoken conversations with people as our eyes met. I looked at a man down in front—a stranger to me—but he diverted his eyes from mine. I persisted until our eyes finally met. I smiled and nodded an almost imperceptible greeting. He began to weep.

After the service he came up to me and apologized for his tears. He said, "It's been so long since anyone smiled at me—I couldn't believe it. It felt so good." He later confessed Christ as his own.

Broken relationships distort the message. We are ministers of reconciliation. Our job is to call men and women to be reconciled to God. God does not need to be reconciled to man; only man needs to be reconciled.

But no one can see our reconciliation to God. Vertical reconciliation is invisible. We can describe it, we can acknowledge that it has happened, but we can't display it.

Our vertical relationship with God is only made visible by our horizontal relationships with people. Jesus said it: "By this all men will know that you are My disciples, if you have love for one another" (John 13:35). Our relationship with God is confirmed by our relationships with people. What an indictment this passage presents to fractured, fragmented, hostile, angry believers who consistently display anything but love to each other. The message of reconciliation is terribly distorted.

I met a man who lived across the street from a church I pastored. I invited him to join us. He looked at me with dismay and said, "You want me to come to that church? I've got enough problems of my own already. All you people do is fight. If I want a fight I can get that at home."

Oneness was the passion of our Lord for Christians. To unite disunited humanity is something only God can do. When that oneness is visible in our relationships, then Jesus' claim to be God is verified and the message of reconciliation comes through loud and clear to those around us who so desperately need to hear it.

Broken relationships restrict our liberty. Years ago I had an angry exchange with a church leader over my resignation. He was convinced that my procedure was wrong. I was convinced that it was right. For the next 20 years there was distance between us and we found that fellowship was impossible. We never resolved our conflict.

Then I was called to become senior pastor of the church where he was a member. I knew that I could not offer my gift of preaching to God from the pulpit as long as he was seated in a pew in front of me. I cannot preach with liberty when I'm party to an unresolved conflict with one of the members of my church or my family. If my relationship with someone in the audience has been fractured and not healed, I cannot comfortably interact with that person in the sermon. The fracture must be healed.

I dreaded the first service when this man and I would see each other and be reminded that things were not right between us. I tried numerous times to contact him. I felt defeated as I entered the church building on that first Sunday in my new role. The fracture had not been healed; the relationship had not been restored.

Then I saw him coming down the hall. He greeted me warmly and welcomed me profusely. I was bewildered. Our last meeting 20 years earlier had been anything but cordial.

We went to my office and I asked him privately, "Do you remember the last time we were together?"

"No," he replied.

"I do," I said. "We had a severe argument. We disagreed violently over the manner in which I resigned. My brother, will you forgive me for offending you?"

He looked at me for a moment, then a slight smile crept over his face. "I do remember," he said finally. "Yes, I forgive you. Will you also forgive me for offending you?"

"Yes," I answered.

We hugged each other and renewed our friendship, and it is deeper and better today than ever. I was finally free to offer my gift to him and my new congregation. Something happens to relationships that pass through the crisis of a major fracture. When they're healed the bond is stronger than ever.

People Above Principles

What I said to my friend that day has always been difficult for me to say. In essence I said,

> I would rather be right with you than be right.

It's not always possible to place relationships above principles. But as I look back at all the disagreements I've had with people over the years, seldom do I see one that merits a breach of friendship. And when I see how important our oneness is to our Lord and how critical it is to proving the credibility of our Savior, oneness takes on even greater importance.

That oneness is so vital that *unity*—not principle—becomes the issue.

That concept is hard for me to put on paper. It's even harder to accept. For people who have been weaned on the importance of principle and the significance of doctrine, to suddenly back down from a position for the purpose of unity is extremely awkward.

It seems downright cowardly.

Jesus suggests that it is not cowardly, but Christian.

That oneness we're preserving and displaying is the loudest Christian sermon that we're ever called upon to share.

That oneness is so important that it even takes priority over worship and even demands that worship be interrupted whenever it's missing.

I preached recently in a service that routinely reversed the order of the morning service. The invocation and opening hymn were followed by the sermon.

The second half of the service included what we usually incorporate in the first half: hymns, choir specials, offering, etc.

After the message I sat in the front row with the pastor. Three times during the singing of worship songs, people slipped out of their seats, walked to the front, and sat alongside their pastor.

They would quietly whisper something to him, and he would respond. They would then move back to their seats.

After the service I asked, "What was that all about?"

"We were just doing what you'd told us to do in your message. We had a very heavy business meeting last week and many of us said things we wished we hadn't. Those people were just interrupting their worship to ask my forgiveness."

". . . First go and be reconciled with your brother . . ."

At the close of a Sunday morning service an elder came forward to ask the church to pray for him.

"Before I can continue to serve the Lord, there's something I must do, and I can't do it unless you pray for me," he said.

We prayed for him.

That evening during the service he asked to speak again. "Thank you for praying for me," he said. "This afternoon I called a former pastor of this church—one whom I ran out of here 22 years ago. I asked him to forgive me—and do you know what he did? He forgave me, and I'm free. Free for the first time in 22 years. Now I can go back to work."

". . . First be reconciled with your brother . . ."

A 14-year-old high school student asked his pastor for bus money. "I've got to go see my father," he explained. "Three years ago my father divorced my

mother. When he left, I told him that I didn't want to
ever see him again. This week I learned that my dad is
dying of cancer. I've got to go and ask his forgiveness."

He went.

He met his dad at the front door and said, "Dad,
can you ever forgive me for what I said to you?"

His dad opened the screen door, took his boy in
his arms, and sobbed, "Son, can you ever forgive me
for what I've done?"

". . . First go and be reconciled to your brother . . ."

A young woman told me her story. Years before,
A young woman told mer her story. Years before,
There was a divorce, followed by marriage. The two
women were in the same church.

Since the divorce they had never spoken to each
other. One sat on one side of the sanctuary, the other
in the opposite corner.

After being reminded of Matthew 5:23 and 24, the
one who had broken up the marriage drove over to the
other woman's house. She stood outside the front
door and sobbed out her apology. "Can you ever forgive me for what I did?"

It took just a few seconds for them to move inside.
They spent the rest of that Sunday afternoon weeping
and praying together as they restored a fractured relationship.

"Do you know what happened tonight?" she
asked. "We sat together in the service."

". . . First be reconciled to your brother . . ."

Human relationships are important to Jesus. He
encourages us to even interrupt our worship of Him if
these relationships are fractured and need healing.

4

The Winsomeness of Oneness

❦

The lonely people of this world—which includes us all—are searching for meaningful relationships.

Jim Millard was 66 years old. His three marriages had ended in failure. His four children were scattered and out of touch. He had never been able to hold onto a job. In desperation he sought freedom from his failures and from himself by living as a recluse in a small prospector's cabin in the Yukon. He shunned interaction with others. He craved privacy. He withdrew completely.

One couple built a small, modestly furnished log cabin about a mile from Jim. The couple had been married 18 years and had no children. They repeatedly invited Jim to dinner. He repeatedly refused. Finally—reluctantly—he accepted. The dinner was satisfying but not spectacular. Yet Jim found the visit to be surprisingly comfortable. He told the story later:

> It was the most disarming thing—difficult to describe and even more difficult to understand. They met me at the door. Each greeted me warmly. As they hung up my gear I sensed the strangest feeling. The only word which could possibly describe it is peace.
>
> We talked comfortably. I felt myself relaxing as I became increasingly aware of the complete

lack of tension in their marriage. Each was his own person and yet each had his own opinions and convictions, but neither tried to impose them on the other or on me. Occasionally they disagreed, but when they did they listened to each other attentively. Sometimes they reached an agreement and sometimes they didn't. But they respected each other's opinions. They were free from intimidation and threat.

They were kind to each other, not as a display to impress their visitor but as a way of life. There was an openness about them, a transparency that allowed each one free access to the thoughts of the other.

They openly discussed their Christianity, not in an attempt to convert me but as a very natural and important part of their lives. As I walked back to my cabin late that night I thought, *If only I had met them sooner. Maybe I could have learned how to love and how to communicate. Maybe I could have saved my marriage and kept my children. Maybe I could have held onto a job. Maybe . . .*

I craved what that couple enjoyed. Months later I asked them to tell me their secret. They did. They simply allowed Jesus Christ to have control of their lives and gave the Holy Spirit access to their marriage. The result was oneness. It was too late for me to recover what I had lost, but it was not too late to change.

Jim found Christ without a church, without a preacher, and even without a Bible. He found Christ in a relationship—a relationship that made Jesus irresistibly attractive to him.

Just before Jesus died, He prayed that man's broken relationship with God and man's broken relationship with man would be restored. His prayer reached beyond the scope of His own generation to include even those of us who live and love and struggle today. He said: "I do not ask in behalf of these alone, but for those also who believe in Me through their Word; that they may all be one; even as Thou, Father, art in Me, and I in Thee, that they also may be in Us; that the world may believe that Thou didst send Me" (John 17:20,21).

Jesus asked His Father to allow us to experience the security, the serenity, the love, and the sheer delight of enjoying one another to the same degree that He and Father God enjoyed each other. He prayed for an indivisible oneness, a timeless union that would penetrate the human heart and soul, creating a oneness between people which reflected the oneness He enjoyed with the Father.

Jesus' prayer was answered in the beginning stages of Christianity when individuals from every nation under heaven were lifted out of their differences to become "of one heart and soul" (Acts 4:32). The meaningful relationships that emerged in those early days in the life of the church transcended all the human barriers that culture and color and language had erected. The early Christians became a first-century phenomenon as hostility, diversity, animosity, and suspicion between them were crushed beneath the weight of their love and unity.

Keith Miller refers to the fragrance emitted by their oneness as "the scent of love." This fragrance was dispensed wherever new Christians were found. It drew a skeptical world away from its hopeless cynicism to find new life and new relationships in Jesus Christ.

The meaningful relationships Jesus prayed for go beyond surface identities. They surpass denominational and doctrinal ties. They exceed ethnic and cultural similarities. They lift people above and beyond racial and physical differences. They establish a bond between individuals who believe that the doctrine of reconciliation with man is included in the doctrine of reconciliation with God.

The Ripple Effect of Oneness

In his book, *The Different Drum*, which deals with the subject of oneness, Dr. M. Scott Peck shares a provocative story which illustrates the benefits of community. The story is thought to be a myth with many versions and is called "The Rabbi's Gift."

The story concerns a monastery which had fallen on hard times. Once it was part of a great order. But persecution in the seventeenth and eighteenth centuries, and the rise of secularism in the nineteenth century, had reduced it to one branch house with only five old monks. Clearly the order was dying.

In the deep woods surrounding the monastery there was a little cabin which an aging rabbi from a nearby town occasionally used for a retreat. During one of the rabbi's retreats, the old abbot from the monastery, agonizing over the imminent death of his order, decided to visit the wise old Jew and ask for advice as to how he might save the monastery.

The rabbi welcomed the abbot to his hut. But when the abbot explained the purpose of his visit the rabbi could only sympathize with him. "I know how it is," he explained. "The spirit has gone out of the people. It is the same in my town. Almost no one comes to the synagogue anymore." So the old abbot and the old rabbi wept together. They read parts of the Torah and quietly spoke of deep things.

When it came time to leave they embraced each other. Then the abbot said, "Is there nothing you can tell me, no piece of advice you can give me that would help save my dying order?"

"No, I'm sorry," the rabbi responded. "I have no advice to give. The only thing I can tell you is that the Messiah is among you."

When the abbot returned to the monastery his fellow monks gathered around him to hear what the rabbi said. "He couldn't help us," the abbot answered sadly. "We just wept and read the Torah together. The only thing he said was that the Messiah is among us. But I don't know what he meant."

In the weeks and months that followed, each monk pondered the rabbi's comment and wondered whether there was any significance to his words. *Could he possibly have meant that one of us here at the monastery is the Messiah? If so, which one? Do you suppose he meant the abbot? Yes, if he meant anyone he meant Father Abbot. He has been our leader for more than a generation.*

On the other hand he might have meant Brother Thomas. Everyone knows that Brother Thomas is a holy man, a man of light.

Certainly he didn't mean Brother Elred! Elred gets crotchety at times. But, come to think of it, even though he's a thorn in our sides, Elred is virtually always right. Maybe the rabbi did mean Brother Elred.

But surely the Messiah is not Brother Philip. Philip is so passive, a real nobody. But then he has a gift for always being there when we need him. Maybe Philip is the Messiah.

Of course the rabbi couldn't possibly have meant me. I'm just an ordinary person. But suppose he did mean me? Suppose I am the Messiah? O God, please not me! I couldn't possibly be Your promised Messiah, could I?

The more they pondered the rabbi's words, the more the old monks treated each other with extraordinary respect, realizing the possibility that one of them might be the Messiah. And each monk began treating himself with extraordinary respect, realizing that he himself might be the Messiah.

Because the monastery was situated in such a beautiful forest, people from the nearby villages still came to picnic on its tiny lawn, to wander along some of its paths. When the villagers encountered the five old monks, they sensed the aura of extraordinary respect which surrounded them and which seemed to radiate from them. There was something strangely attractive—even compelling about the relationship between them.

Without really knowing why, people began returning to the monastery more frequently to picnic and to play. They began to bring their friends to this special place. And their friends brought other friends.

Eventually some of the younger men who came to visit began talking with the old monks. Soon one young man asked if he could join their order. Within a few years the monastery was once again a thriving order and, thanks to the rabbi's gift, a vibrant center of light and spirituality.[1]

Once in Italy I told this story to a group of Protestant missionaries and then closed the meeting without any further discussion. Some were quite offended. One of them said, "It's interesting that a Baptist pastor has traveled all the way to Naples to tell Protestant missionaries how to rebuild dying Catholic churches."

Another one asked, "How could the Messiah ever be found in a monastery?"

Another missionary blustered, "Since when do we seek advice from a Jewish rabbi?"

Another interjected, "I thought the Messiah had already come."

Still another added, "We don't have to ask anybody how to revive dying churches. The Bible tells us all we need to know."

I share this story often and usually the response is much better. I use it to launch discussions on the subject of oneness. "What is this parable saying to us?" I often begin. Here are some of the most common responses:

> We need to learn how to love each other.

> We need to learn how to respect each other.

> We need to realize that the Messiah is already among us.

> If we treated each other as we ought, maybe the world would be more interested in our message.

> If we were constantly aware of the presence of the indwelling Christ, we would act differently.

> Christ is always present. Our words and our thoughts should be controlled by this reality.

> It sounds a little frightening to me. It tells me that the reason Christianity is so unattractive today is us.

One man, who was sitting in the back of the little Sunday School class I was teaching, waited until everyone was finished commenting. Then he beamed, "It sounds like a revival to me."

The monks in the story had much in common: their history, their dogma, their traditions, their clerical garb, their rituals, their schedules, their residence, their titles, their library, and the fact that they lived together and shared everything. But they were not experiencing oneness. And their lack of oneness nullified the dynamic of their commonness and negated the dynamic of their ministry. But when their commonness was replaced by community, they were revived and so was the little world around them.

A Baptism of Oneness

I have often wondered where my mind would have been if I had been among the group of 120 gathered in their upper room in Jerusalem just prior to the Day of Pentecost (Acts 1). I probably would have been terribly distracted during those ten days of waiting. I'm an activist. I usually try to solve a problem before I even fully understand it. I attack first and then try to develop my strategy. I seldom read an instruction manual. I just set about doing the job—and often fail.

During those ten days following Jesus' ascension into heaven, I would have been anxious to get to the task just assigned to me: preaching the gospel to every creature. I would have chafed under the pressure of a never-ending prayer meeting. The monumental job of reaching the world didn't need a ten-day time lag; it needed full and immediate attention.

I would have attacked the mandate given me by Jesus with all the strength and wisdom at my disposal—and would have accomplished nothing. I would not have known how to do it.

My questions would have been many. How can a handful of unknown semi-literates impact a hostile world that doesn't even realize it has a need? How can provincial minds which never crossed the borders of their nation—one of the earth's smallest—suddenly become cosmopolitan and embrace the whole world? How can a dozen men, limited to the crude dialect of the Galileans, make themselves understood in the hundreds of languages of earth? How can a few unpolished members of an outcast nation gain the respectful attention of disbelieving, disinterested worldlings and ultimately direct them toward repentance and faith in Jesus Christ? How can the world's first church leaders, working without the benefit of a shelf full of church growth books, establish and grow a church that will ultimately invade every stratum of society?

God, in a strategic moment of time, did all of the above and more—and He did it in a time-honored fashion. He employed a strategy that works as well in the twentieth and twenty-first centuries as it did in the first. He caused strangers from different cultures and races, speaking different languages, to love and respect each other.

For 1,500 years before Jesus came, the sons of Israel practiced a ritual they never fully understood. At the feast of first fruits they bound individual stalks of grain together and waved them before the Lord (Leviticus 23:9-14). This feast symbolized the resurrection of Christ (1 Corinthians 15:23). For 1,500 years the sons of Israel announced through ritual that Christ would be the first to rise from the dead.

Fifty days after the feast of first fruits, during the feast of Pentecost, the Jews ground the kernels from those stalks of grain into fine flour and baked bread. By doing so they proclaimed that, 50 days after the Messiah's resurrection, He would form a company comprised of individuals who would lose their identities to one another, just as the separate heads of grain lost their identity to the loaf.

On the day of Pentecost, 50 days after Christ's resurrection, 120 individual believers, loosely bound together by faith in their Master's promise, ascended the steps to that upper room. On that day the Holy Spirit of God mystically united them into one homogeneous living organism: the body of Christ. One hundred and twenty individuals went up those stairs, one body—the church—came down. One hundred and twenty separate identities, separate cultures, separate languages, separate backgrounds, separate convictions, and separate traditions were poured together into the mystical mold of oneness; a whole new being emerged. The community of the Spirit was formed.

Before the sun set on the day of Pentecost, the community of 120 swelled to about 3,000 (Acts 2:41). And remember: These new believers were very different from each other. They were from the four corners of the known world—Mesopotamia to the east, Rome to the west, Asia to the north, and Ethiopia to the south. They were isolated, alienated, fragmented, lonely people who as yet didn't understand why they were lonely. These were the representative "insecures" of the earth who, in a strange country, in even stranger surroundings, among people of a strange language, suddenly and inexplicably were at peace with God, themselves, and each other. This was the genius of the Holy Spirit of God. This was the miracle of the Book of Acts.

In his book, *The Scent of Love*, Keith Miller reminds us that evangelism takes on many forms. But one method that is often neglected is the one God used so profoundly in the city of Jerusalem after the birth of the church. Miller says:

> When these Christians, filled with the Spirit, got together, they formed tiny outposts of the kingdom throughout the Roman world. They opened their lives to each other, they helped each other with personal problems and all kinds of difficulties. They prayed together, read the Scriptures and regularly shared the thanksgiving meal which developed later into what was called the Lord's Supper. . . . These outposts of the kingdom were exciting places into which the early church members brought people to meet their Lord, to be healed and to be made new.

And when pagans made a deep contact with Christians, they became different. They found a new way to live in a world which had been a frustrating chaos for them. They too were faced with problems like high interest rates, deterioration of family, anxiety about the future and death. But now they could deal with these and other problems with a peace and a sense of fulfillment they never dreamed they could have. And they felt loved and forgiven—free to love others and free to love people and tell them the news.[2]

The Winsomeness of Oneness Wins

The four young men were dropouts from the civilized world as we know it. They did not know each other. Each had completed his schooling, entered the business world, and had been fairly successful—only to be disillusioned and unfulfilled. Each had left an eastern seaboard state to lose himself in the Alaskan frontier. Each was running away from a broken marriage. They all settled in the wilderness north of Fairbanks where they eventually met and became friends.

One of these young men was confronted with the claims of Christ by a bush pilot who landed his ski-equipped plane near his cabin. The young man had no sooner received Christ than he sent for the wife he had deserted, led her to Christ, and they proceeded to rebuild their marriage.

The second young man, who lived nearby, witnessed the change in his friend and noticed the emerging peace and serenity of his marriage. He also accepted Christ. In turn he sent for his wife, who was already a Christian, and they began rebuilding their marriage.

The third man was so obviously impressed by the changes he saw in his friends that he too accepted Christ and urged his wife to join him in Alaska. With the help of their new Christian brothers and sisters, this third couple also set about rebuilding their broken marriage.

I realize that the story is filled with a delightful sort of monotony, but I must tell you that the fourth young man had the same experience. He found Christ by watching the others. He also experienced a reunited, restored, and happy marriage.

I talked to three of these four men personally. Each recounted the story above in much greater detail than I have told it to you. "What are your plans now?" I asked them.

"We're looking for a fifth—another man who needs to find Jesus and find himself. After that we'll just keep looking for more."

There's redemptive influence in a meaningful relationship. Jesus makes oneness possible and He intends to use the fragrance of these relationships to make His message irresistibly attractive to the lonely of this world.

5

Immersed in the Community of the Spirit

❦

Recently my secretary placed on my desk a "Peanuts" comic strip featuring Charlie Brown. In the first frame Charlie swings his bat and misses the ball for strike two. With grim determination he faces the pitcher, takes another swing, and, as usual, strikes out. Dejectedly he trudges out of the batter's box dragging his bat behind him.

He walks up to Lucy, throws down his bat, and says, "Rats! I'll never be a big-league player! I just don't have it. All my life I've dreamed of playing in the big leagues. But now I know I'll never make it."

"You're thinking too far ahead, Charlie Brown," Lucy says. "What you need is to set some immediate goals."

Charlie's face looks puzzled. "Immediate goals?" he asks.

"Yes, immediate goals," Lucy says. "For instance, start with this next inning when you go out to pitch. See if you can walk out to the mound without falling down."

As a pastor, I also have struggled with goals and priorities in ministering to the Christian community. Like Charlie Brown, my driving ambition for years was to play in the big leagues. From the beginning—

as carnal as it may sound—I wanted to be the successful pastor of a growing church. I wanted to be well
known, highly esteemed, and in great demand as a
spiritual leader.

Little did I realize that I knew nothing about this
wonderfully mysterious living organism called the
church, to say nothing of knowing how to make it
grow. Call me Charlie Brown. I didn't even know how
to walk out to the mound.

For years I struggled with priorities until one
simple passage of Scripture leaped out at me. Jesus
was teaching some significant truths about the kingdom of God and how it grows. He said: "The kingdom
of God is like a man who casts seed upon the ground;
and goes to bed at night and gets up by day, and the
seed sprouts up and grows—how, he himself does not
know. The earth produces crops by itself; first the
blade, then the head, then the mature grain in the
head. But when the crop permits, he immediately puts
in the sickle, because the harvest has come" (Mark
4:26-29).

It became obvious to me that my responsibility
was not to produce growth. That's something that
happens apart from anything I can do. Like the farmer, I can plant seed and I can harvest the crop, but I
can't cause growth. And like the farmer, I can't even
explain the mystery of a sprouting seed.

All the farmer knows about producing growth is
that the life of the seed is in the seed. That's all I need
to know about growing the church. The life of the
living church is in the church. Given the chance, it will
grow by itself. My job, like the farmer's, is to create an
environment that's conducive to growth. As a farmer
tills and waters the soil and removes the weeds, so I'm
to preserve an environment that's free of suspicion,
tension, threat, anger, and bitterness so human relationships can flourish. My responsibility is to preach,

pray, and practice in such a manner that a living, loving body of believers may experience and display an environment of oneness which is comfortable to those within and attractive to those without.

Relationships Result in Growth

Let me say it again: Christians are the only company of people in all the world privileged to experience meaningful relationships—an experience that's designed to dispel loneliness and distance. Only Christians can enjoy complete and continuing reconciliation between God and man, between man and man, and between man and woman. This meaningful oneness, which the apostle Paul calls "the unity of the Spirit" (Ephesians 4:3), is the most attractive commodity Christians have to offer a fractured world. Our job is to make the preservation of the unity of the Spirit our highest goal. When we do that, God will take care of the growth of our community.

Where meaningful and fulfilling relationships are present, churches grow. Where they are absent, the churches decline.

Christians need to project a new image—which really isn't new at all—to the world. It's the image which was displayed in the Book of Acts and is occasionally seen in small pockets of believers today. It's the image which is visible in China. Twenty years of repression have caused the church there to grow from one million to more than 50 million vibrant believers.

The image needed is an environment of caring, sharing, loving, and listening. It's a climate of meaningful relationships in Christian communities that will satisfy humanity's lingering loneliness.

If we're going to meet the world's need, we Christians must become more like Julie's description in chapter 1:

People who are bonded together.

People who love each other as much as we claim to love Christ.

People who care for each other and share with each other.

People who are learning to communicate honestly with each other.

People whose relationships go deeper than the masks of their composure.

People who are committed to each other.

People who allow each other—
the freedom to fail, and
the freedom to succeed, and
the freedom to weep, and
the freedom to rejoice, and
the freedom to be different.

We do want truth and holiness. We do want meaning for life. But we need to be Christians who value relationships as much as theology and who place people above projects. We need to be Christians who understand the priority of meaningful relationships and who are willing to pay the price to develop and preserve them.

The Gospel of Oneness

Relationships are part of the gospel. That's a little threatening to those who may have never thought about it before. The gospel is usually identified as "the power of God for salvation to everyone who believes, to the Jew first and also to the Greek" (Romans 1:16). We often see the gospel only as God going one-on-one with individuals.

Similarly, those of us who have grown up under the influence of modern-day evangelicalism, fundamentalism, Wesleyan holiness teaching, or Pentecostalism have all viewed the work of the Holy Spirit as a private experience necessary for empowering the individual for personal piety and witness.

But according to the Book of Acts, relationships were at the heart of the outpouring of the Holy Spirit and the subsequent proclamation of the gospel. Pentecost was not a private experience; Pentecost was a corporate experience. We're told in Acts that (emphases added):

> A gathering of about *one hundred and twenty persons* were there *together* (1:15);
>
> *They* put forward two men (1:23);
>
> *They* prayed (1:24);
>
> *They* drew lots (1:26);
>
> *They* were all *together* in one place (2:1);
>
> A noise like a violent, rushing wind... filled the house where *they* were sitting (2:2);
>
> There appeared to *them* tongues as of fire... and they rested on each one of *them* (2:3);
>
> *They* were *all* filled with the Holy Spirit and began to speak with other tongues, as the Spirit was giving *them* utterance (2:4);
>
> When this sound occurred, the multitude came together, and were bewildered, because they were each one hearing *them* speak in his own language (2:6).

Pentecost was not the experience of one individual being supernaturally invaded by the Holy Spirit. Pentecost was the experience of the Spirit of God giving birth to one body which was comprised of 120 individuals.

In Acts 1:4 the disciples were warned not to preach the gospel until the Holy Spirit came upon them. Why? Not only were they to wait for the empowering of the Holy Spirit, but they were to wait because the gospel they were to preach had not yet been completed. The individual followers of Christ had not yet been melted together and molded into His body the church by the fire of the Holy Spirit.

C. Norman Krause describes Pentecost as the climax of a three-act drama. Act one was the incarnation of God in the body of Christ which continued through the years of His earthly ministry. Act two was the passion of Christ when Jesus took upon Himself the sins of the whole world. Act three was Pentecost when the promise of the Father was fulfilled and the new body, the church, was formed (Luke 24:49; Acts 1:4).[1]

The disciples were not just to wait for the Spirit's arrival in Jerusalem, but also for the formation of the new body through which Christ would continue to expand His presence and ministry. Just as the people of Israel received their new identity as the people of God at Sinai through the gift of the law, so the new people of God, called the church, was constituted through the gift of the Spirit.

Baptized into Belonging

That moment of the believers' identification with the body of Christ is called the baptism of the Holy Spirit. The apostle Paul described the Spirit's baptism in 1 Corinthians 12:13: "For by one Spirit we were all baptized into one body, whether Jews or Greeks, whether slaves or free, and we were all made to drink of one Spirit." What is the baptism of the Holy Spirit? Dr. Charles Ryrie says: "Baptism is a form of identification. . . . The baptism with the Holy Spirit . . . identifies members of the body of Christ with Christ, the risen head of that body."[2]

The Bible teaches that the baptism of the Holy Spirit is that mystical experience by which a believer is supernaturally immersed into the body of Christ. Personal identity is lost as one is submerged into a greater identity. He becomes vitally and inseparably joined together with the millions of others of like belief and with Jesus who is the head of the body.

Spirit baptism takes place at the moment of conversion. There is no conversion without it (Romans 8:9). The original baptism into oneness took place at Pentecost and continues every time a new believer is added to the ever-expanding body of Christ.

The great achievement of God at Pentecost—the great moment for which the disciples were to wait—was the moment when community was restored. God and man, who had been separated since the garden of Eden, were reunited. Man and man, who had been separated since Babel, were again one.

The great miracle of God at Pentecost was meaningful relationships—oneness both vertically and horizontally. The gift of tongues was just one of the tools God used to produce that miracle.

The baptism of the Spirit of God is the means by which meaningful relationships are made possible. The oneness which results is the identifying mark of the Spirit's baptism—the Christian's I.D. badge. Oneness is our unique and distinctive trademark. Oneness is the genius of God designed to satisfy the deep need of lonely, fragmented, fractured humanity.

Oneness for All and
All for Oneness

Since the day of Pentecost, salvation has meant receiving Christ, experiencing forgiveness of sins, being indwelt by the Holy Spirit, being baptized, and becoming a member of the Christian community. The church (*ekklesia*, meaning "called out ones") has been called out from the world to be ushered into something new: the community of the Spirit.

And since Pentecost, individual believers are no longer autonomous or complete in themselves. We only experience wholeness or completeness in relationships with one another. Salvation not only means to be organically and inseparably united to Christ, it also means to be organically and inseparably united with fellow humans under the lordship of Christ (1 Corinthians 12:12-14). Krause says: "Modern insights from anthropology, sociology and psychology confirm the biblical presupposition that the basic human unit is not the independent individual before God, but the individual-in-community before God."[3]

Relationships between believers are central in the epistles of Paul. To the Philippians Paul appealed for a spirit of servanthood and unselfishness based on the "fellowship [*koinonia*] of the Spirit" as evidence of the new oneness (Philippians 2:1-11). To the Galatians and Colossians he stressed that being "in Christ" meant that all sexual, racial, economic, social, and cultural barriers between believers were eliminated (Galatians 3:26-28; Colossians 3:9-11). To the Corinthians he taught that sharing financial assistance was part of the responsibility of oneness (1 Corinthians 16:1-4).

According to the New Testament, service (Romans 12:6-8), hospitality (1 Peter 4:9), discipline (1 Corinthians 5), and *agape* love (1 Corinthians 13) are to characterize the relationships that exist in the new community. Furthermore, the community of the Spirit is to be marked by peace between believers (Romans 14:17). Peace is what makes the community of believers so irresistibly attractive to the hostiles of humanity. The Christian community is the only group in the world offering peace—peace with God and peace with man—to all who unite.

The community of the Spirit is where our oneness is made visible. Oneness is the genius of God and the strategy of the Holy Spirit. Oneness is Christianity in action and *koinonia* on display. Oneness is the miracle of the Book of Acts and the glory of the New Testament church today.

Oneness with God and man through Christ is the completion of the gospel. In Christ my sins are forgiven forever. And in the Christian community my loneliness and alienation are forever abolished.

PART II

❦

Profile of a
Meaningful Relationship

6

Just the Way You Are

❦

Healthy relationships have certain definable characteristics. Each characteristic by itself may seem like a fragile thread. But when woven together with great care they comprise a fabric of strength in the community of the Spirit which is permanent, indestructible, and disarmingly attractive to the lonely who are looking on from the outside.

The characteristics which constitute the profile of a meaningful relationship must be both present and visible in Christ's body. Jesus prayed that these characteristics would be displayed in us in such a fashion that our relationships would give credibility to His claim to be the Son of God.

Meaningful relationships are meant to satisfy us, but they are also meant for the eyes of others. We need to experience the oneness these characteristics implement for our own health, but we also need to communicate our oneness to a fractured, fragmented world.

Acceptance with No Exceptions

Meaningful relationships must be accepting.

Two men served effectively together in a church I pastored until one learned that the other drank wine.

The nondrinker resigned his position claiming he could no longer serve together with a drinker.

As the three of us met together I shared with them the contents of Romans 14. To the one who was critical I read, "Who are you to judge the servant of another?" (Romans 14:4). I asked him, "Are you judging your brother in the use of wine?"

"Yes," he nodded.

"Do you have a clear biblical right to judge him in that matter?"

"No."

To the other I read, "Therefore let us not judge one another anymore, but rather determine this—not to put an obstacle or a stumbling block in a brother's way" (Romans 4:13). I asked, "Is your wine an offense or an obstacle to your brother?"

"It seems like it is," he admitted.

To them both I said, "It seems like one of you is judging and the Scriptures say not to, and the other is offending and again the Scriptures say not to. Now what are you two going to do?"

They both thought for a long time. Finally one approached the other and said, "Will you forgive me for judging you?"

The other answered, "Yes," and added, "Will you forgive me for offending you?"

"Yes."

The one stopped being critical and the other stopped drinking, and together they went back to work.

Oneness is built on acceptance with no exceptions. We cannot exclude the poor, the doubters, the sinners, or people of different sex, race, or nationality. To reject a child because he fails to measure up to parental expectations, a wife because she doesn't meet a husband's requirements, or a parent because of aging is foreign to the teachings of Jesus. Our Lord displayed a remarkable open-door policy to all:

> To lepers, who were the first-century equivalents of people with AIDS;
>
> To criminals like Matthew and Zaccheus;
>
> To adulterers like the one about to be stoned;
>
> To the wealthy like the rich young ruler;
>
> To the young like the little children who gathered around him;
>
> To the powerful like the Jewish rabbi Nicodemus;
>
> To the oppressive like the Roman centurion whose child He healed;
>
> To the opposition like Jairus whose daughter He restored to life;
>
> To the betrayer like Judas who ultimately caused His death.

Jesus was soundly criticized for His acceptance of all who were unacceptable to the narrow bigotry of rigid first-century Judaism.

Acceptance is required in Christian relationships. The apostle Paul said: "Now accept the one who is weak in faith, but not for the purpose of passing judgment on his opinions" (Romans 14:1). Acceptance is a characteristic of the Christian life (Ephesians 4:1,2). It addresses such divisive attitudes as racism, sexism, bigotry, and bias. It ignores color barriers, language barriers, cultural barriers, and economic barriers. It accepts all who accept Christ.

In my book, *Beyond Rejection*, I described my great antipathy toward the homosexual community until I learned that one of my dearest friends was gay. I was confronted with a problem. Would I continue to reject homosexuals or would I limit my rejection only to homosexuality. I chose to continue to hate homosexuality but to do my utmost to help the struggling homosexual who was seeking freedom from his destructive habit. Today members of the gay community call me regularly seeking help. I delight in helping them.

Acceptance is neither critical nor insensitive. It is inclusive of people and only exclusive of sin.

Acceptance Without Words

Acceptance begins in the eyes. When I'm meeting a stranger, I try to never conclude that initial greeting until our eyes have made meaningful contact. Often I greet strangers without engaging in any significant conversation. All we may say to one another is "Good morning" or "Good evening" or "Hi" or "Hello." But I will always engage their eyes. Other strangers will thank me for the sermon I've just delivered. They will shake my hand as they pass, intending to move on. But I don't release their hand until our eyes have met.

This is startling to those who are accustomed to quick and usually meaningless handshakes. They begin to withdraw their hand from mine and are surprised that I don't let go. They lift their face with a slightly startled look and eventually our eyes will meet. That eye contact will be very brief—sometimes less than a second. But in that brief moment of time I will communicate my acceptance of them.

The acceptance I convey will be in the form of warmth, interest, concern, openness, and love. I do not look above them, behind them, or beside them. I don't look at their hair, their clothes, their shoes, their jewelry, or what they're carrying in their hands. I look into their eyes. In those eyes I can read pain, confusion, rejection, distraction, or distrust. I can also read peace, contentment, acceptance, interest, and confidence. I'm a firm believer in the idea, "The eyes of men converse as much as their tongues, with the advantage that the ocular dialect needs no dictionary, but is understood the world over."[1]

I can build upon what I see in someone's eyes, and I often do. A sidelong glance, a downcast eye, a drooping eyelid, a blank stare, blinking, gaze aversion, and exaggerated opening of the eye all carry silent messages upon which I can begin a conversation. Often I'll say to a stranger whose eyes are filled with pain, "Can I be of any help to you?" and often their reply allows me the privilege of entering into their life.

Our body language often signals our acceptance or rejection of someone long before any words are spoken. Gestures like folded arms, crossed legs, squinting, peering over the glasses, and tilting the head forward usually suggest suspicion, uncertainty, or rejection. Greeting a stranger with our feet or body pointing to the exit or our eyes shifting to our watch suggests that we want to end that meeting and leave. One of the most rejecting nonverbal messages I encounter is when people talk to me while their eyes are carrying on conversations elsewhere.

Our smiles attract and our frowns repel. If people have to choose between our words and our actions to determine our sincerity, they will always choose our actions. Acceptance is conveyed through warm eyes, a friendly smile, an energetic handshake, and a few moments without distraction.

The Needs of Relationship

Accepting relationships begins with a sense of need. I learned this early in my ministry thanks to a meaningful encounter with a man named M.L.

As a young pastor I regularly attended a men's prayer breakfast. There were about a dozen men who met first to pray and then go out to breakfast.

The prayer time was fairly predictable. One of the men would read a verse or two from the Scriptures and then ask for prayer requests. When we finished voicing our requests we prayed. Each man would take his turn, trying to remember to cover all the requests. After we prayed we adjourned to the local pancake house.

That's when the fun began. We'd laugh and talk and joke with each other until it was time for everyone to go to work. I often wondered what motivated each of us to come. I seriously questioned whether it was the rather mechanical prayer time or the breakfast which caused us to get up and out early in the morning.

Then I met M.L. We were both beginning our careers. He was a young doctor and I was a young pastor. In the middle of our light hearted men's breakfast one morning, M.L. looked across the table at me and, in dead seriousness, asked, "Will you be my friend?"

Without thinking through the implications of his request I answered, "Certainly."

We waited until the other men were gone, then began discussing our professional loneliness. We were each surrounded by a host of people who knew us and loved us. But we admitted to each other that we craved a relationship of intimacy and accountability which we hadn't found in the larger group.

We agreed to meet each Tuesday morning at 6:30 for breakfast. We established a nonthreatening format. I wouldn't come as his pastor and he wouldn't come as my doctor. We would bring our Bibles and relate something we read during the week. We'd share needs with each other and we'd pray. All of this would take place while we ate and we would conclude by 8:00 A.M.

It was fun from the outset. We were about the same age and quite compatible. Our families were small, our careers were far from flourishing, and our needs were quite similar.

We were clumsy at first. Its seems like we spent most of our time just getting acquainted. Our Bible discussions were profitable but our prayer times were somewhat shallow. It took a long time for us to move beneath surface needs to discuss matters of the heart.

Then one day M.L. said, "Don, I need some help. Doctors are never supposed to admit to their ignorance, but I'm baffled. I have a patient who's ill and I can't figure out what's wrong with her. I've conferred with specialists in various fields and they're as confused as I am. I really don't know what to do and I'm too proud to admit it. Will you pray for me? I'm not sure what to pray about first: my pride or my confusion. But right now I need help for both."

I felt wonderfully honored. No doctor had ever asked me to pray in that manner. It seemed like I had just been invited into some inner chamber of human life that I had never visited before.

Then M.L. prayed, "Father, I'm so sinfully proud. It's awfully hard for me to ask for help from anybody, even You. Please forgive me and help me know how to help this hurting little lady. In Jesus' name, amen."

M.L.'s boldness to reveal his need spurred me to open myself also. I prayed, "Father, I have the same problem as M.L. I'm so proud. Forgive me. I need You to help me understand and minister to the hurting people I serve." Then I proceeded to ask God to honor M.L.'s request.

That morning was a breakthrough in our relationship. We met at a point of common need. We expressed a weakness we had both previously tried to hide. We held our weakness up to each other and then up to God.

We both felt a sense of relief. Neither of us shamed the other, judged the other, or rejected the other. We accepted each other for who and where we were. We felt comfortable with each other and experienced peace. We had begun moving in the direction of a meaningful, accepting relationship.

My relationship with M.L. lasted nearly 25 years. We knew each other's strengths, weaknesses, failures, successes, dreams, and goals. The more we knew about each other, the more we needed each other. And the more we needed each other, the more we accepted each other.

We interrupted our prayer breakfasts for seven years when I accepted a pastorate in central California. During those years we often phoned each other.

When I was hospitalized with a major depression, M.L. called. I picked up my bedside phone and heard his voice on the other end of the line: "Hello, Don. This is M.L." The only other words we spoke were our good-byes. The rest of the time was spent crying with each other. It was the most therapeutic phone call I ever received.

Acceptance at the Point of Need

A pastor's wife sat down in a restaurant recently and said to Martha and me, "I've had it. I can't stand it any longer. I just have to get away. My husband preaches his heart out. I give and give until I can't give anymore. All we get in return is criticism. Do you know how I feel? I feel like telling them all to forget it!"

Her language was actually a little more colorful than that, but her frustrations are the same ones shared by many pastors' wives. She has a need.

A couple bordering on retirement are traveling constantly in their business. When they are able to attend their home church they're treated as strangers. They have a need.

Bill and Roberta have been highly motivated, successful business people all their lives. But their once-prosperous business has just failed. They're heavily in debt. Worse yet, they're deeply embarrassed. They have spent their lives giving to others, now they're forced to receive help and don't know how. They have a need.

Jim's wife left him. He doesn't believe he should remarry, but he's lonely. Jim has a need.

George and Helen have a nephew dying from AIDS. They want their church to pray for him but they're afraid to make his condition known. They have a need.

Marion is humiliated because her husband has fallen in love with another woman. She has no one to whom she can go to receive counsel or support. She has a need.

Vicki is depressed. She's been told that depression is a sin so she decides to carry her fear and guilt, along with her unpredictable mood swings, all by herself. She has a need.

Ed and Virginia just received word that their children are returning from the mission field because the culture shock and loneliness were more than they could handle. Ed and Virginia were so proud when they left. Now they're finding it hard to explain to themselves and others why their children are giving up on the ministry. They have a need.

Martha and I have given our lives to local churches. Now we don't have a home church of our own. To be without a home base is a new and lonely experience. We have a need.

Christians who are interested only in evangelism, discipleship, or even worship are failing in their purpose. People are the business of the Christian community—not just the people outside the church, but the people inside as well, not just the new believers, but the old believers also.

Needs are everywhere. Meeting people at their point of need and accepting them where they are is a major step in developing the meaningful relationships which will broadcast our oneness to a hurting world. No wonder the early church grew so rapidly. Their oneness was highly visible because, "There was not a needy person among them" (Acts 4:34). That sense of oneness was a powerful evangelistic tool that made Christians irresistibly attractive to the needy world. That sense of open, accepting oneness must be renewed and revived in today's needy world.

7

Committed to Community

❦

Meaningful relationships require commitment.

Commitment is an act of the will which ignores likes and dislikes. Commitment is the only way human differences can be absorbed in a relationship. Commitment rejects prejudices and personal feelings and determines to achieve the goal of a meaningful relationship whatever the cost. A meaningful relationship is like a marriage. It requires that we hang in there even when the going gets tough.

Commitment is the spirit that prevailed in the early church: "They were continually devoting themselves to the apostles' teaching and to fellowship, to the breaking of bread and to prayer" (Acts 2:42). "Continually devoting themselves" is a tremendous concept of commitment. Those first Christians matched their commitment to Christ with a deep commitment to each other. They did not take their new life lightly. A believer didn't join with fellow-Christians like a person joins a club just to drop in when he felt like it. When the community of the Spirit was formed in Jerusalem it meant something life-changing, something so important that it deserved and demanded total commitment.

Committed to Spiritual Life

The Christian community committed itself to being together for spiritual activities such as teaching, fellowship, the breaking of bread, and prayer. Bible teaching, which is vital to the life of any congregation, was a group activity in the New Testament church. Copies of the Old Testament scrolls were precious and few, as were the epistles. Individual copies were not available. The Scriptures were read aloud in the congregation. If you wanted to hear God's Word in the early church you had to gather with the community. Even though Christians today can study their Bibles alone at home, we still need to commit ourselves to meet together for teaching and learning.

Fellowship was also vital for the survival of individual Christians. The early believers experienced much persecution for their radical belief and bold proclamation that Jesus Christ was the Messiah. They needed each other for encouragement and support as they carried out Christ's commission. Persecution today may not be as severe for most western Christians, but we still need to be together for the revitalization of fellowship.

The breaking of bread referred to the communion service. Communion is an act of worship which is not optional and which is not to be done in private. It is a family celebration continued through the generations by commandment and designed to elevate the living Christ to a point of constant remembrance. The communion service is a rallying place for all believers where they continue to tell the world that Jesus died for us in order that He might live in us.

Many years ago I gave up practicing an abbreviated communion service that was an add-on to another time of worship. I began giving an entire Sunday evening to it each month. It became an anticipated time of celebration for our congregation. When we gave communion its rightful place and committed ourselves to celebrate it wholeheartedly, it gave us rich rewards. It bound us to Jesus. It bound us to each other. It strengthened the spirit of oneness.

The early church was also continually devoted to prayer. Nothing in the Christian life demands a higher level of commitment than prayer. The word "prayers" in Acts 2:42 covers the entire subject of prayer. In the New Testament there are ten different words for prayer. There is one word that means asking, as a poor man asks with empty hands trusting only in the grace of God to fill them. There is another word that means demanding, on the basis of having fulfilled all the conditions for making the request. There are words that suggest a conversational type of prayer, praise, petition, confession, and thanksgiving.

The prayers of the committed early Christians were personal, intimate, and all-inclusive. It usually takes weeks for a group to begin to reach beyond the usual nonthreatening requests to pray about personal needs. It's always an encouraging sign when someone meekly says, "Will you pray for me. I lost my job today" or "My wife and I are struggling to get along together" or "I really don't want to be here tonight; my spirit's all dried up and I need prayer" or "Our son is hooked on drugs. Please pray for us."

That's the kind of praying that is typical of the community of the Spirit as it begins experiencing the spirit of oneness through commitment.

Committed to Stay Together

Being continually devoted suggests a commitment to stay together, worship together, and work together over the long haul. In my pastoral staff, oneness only began to develop after I committed myself to no less than ten years as their senior pastor. It's the same principle that applies in marriage when "till death us do part" is taken seriously. When you're committed to stay you don't run away at the first sign of trouble.

My friend Stu Weber pastors a rapidly growing community of Christians in Boring, Oregon. A bottom-line attitude he maintains toward his staff and his people is captured in their motto: "Nothing shall divide us." That kind of commitment creates an environment where relationships can grow.

People who are committed to long-term, meaningful relationships accept the fact that wise decisions can best be made in a group. One person alone is seriously limited in the decision-making process. It took me a long time to admit that I didn't know all the answers. A super-sized ego often caused me to close my ears to the wisdom of others.

Whenever there was a crisis in the first-century church, the early Christians went into a huddle. This was not to deny the presence of the all-wise Spirit of God in each individual member. It was to protect Christians from the tendency to filter that wisdom only through their individual experience or understanding.

When persecution arose among the Christians, they met together for strength (Acts 4:13-23). When internal conflict arose, they met together to seek a solution (Acts 6:1-7). When confusion arose, they met together for wisdom (Acts 15:1-21). When a decision was reached, they met together for the announcement (Acts 15:30,31).

Committed relationships accept the limitations of individualism and seek the counsel of others. A committed believer shares his burdens and decisions with at least one other person who really cares.

In my pastorates, one of my first requests of the governing boards was, "Please, people, keep me from making a fool of myself. If my suggestions seem fool-ish, please say so." My church staffs became so im-portant to me in the process of making decisions that I eventually would consider nothing of significance without the corporate wisdom of the men and women who served with me. I've learned through experience the truth of Proverbs 12:15: "A wise man is he who listens to counsel."

One of the stark contrasts between the Old and New Testaments is found in this concept of God speak-ing to people. In the Old Testament, God spoke to individuals. When it was time for Abraham to move his loved ones from their family home in ancient Ur of the Chaldees, God issued His command directly to Abraham and no one else (Genesis 12:1-3).

But in the New Testament God spoke to individ-uals through the group. When it was time for the apostle Paul to leave the comforts of ancient Antioch and begin his itinerate missionary tours, God spoke to Paul through the church (Acts 13:1-3).

Stark reality suggests that there is safety in num-bers. Human limitation demands that I admit my needs to you, ask you to help me process my prob-lems, and depend on you to assist me in arriving at solutions. This feature of meaningful relationships can best be served when we are continually devoted to each other.

Committed to Talk

People committed to meaningful relationships
talk to each other,
become vulnerable to each other,
honestly acknowledge their fears,
openly confess their faults,
discuss life and death, and
they even talk about Jesus.

In other words, their conversations go deeper than the Daytona 500, the stock market, the latest fashions, or the cost of living.

In committing themselves to each other, the early Christians didn't meet just to study the Bible and pray, but also to look into each other's eyes and talk about the inner life. That's a terribly threatening thing to most people today, but it's necessary to experiencing the spirit of oneness.

Gil Beers says that the most prized gift of all the gifts given to man is the gift of talk. I like that. And I like the fact that he uses the word "talk" in place of the clinical word "communication." I also like the fact that he distinguishes between meaningless and meaningful talk: "Each of us has a longing to talk meaningfully, purposefully, and redemptively with each other. We want to talk so that others will listen and will feel uplifted and revitalized when they do. I think we have a desire to enhance one another without conversation, but I know of very few people who practice that gift."[1]

Did you notice that Gil Beers makes the distinction between talking *to* and talking *with*? There is quite a difference. Talking *with* should be our goal. Let me make some suggestions about exercising the gift of talking with people.

1. Talking with people means learning their names. I can never concentrate on a conversation if I'm unsure of a person's name. I give my name first—"Hi, I'm Don Baker." They usually respond with their name. If I don't hear it, I ask them to repeat it. If I'm still unsure of the pronunciation, I'll ask them to spell it. If the name suggests a foreign nationality, I'll ask them, "Is that German?" or "Is that Welsh?"

Asking people about their names does two things. First, it helps lock the name into my memory. Second, it often provides a transition into another topic of interest, like, "I know some Andersons in Minneapolis. What part of the country are you from?"

I feel that I don't really know people if I don't know their names. And they feel that I am not interested in them if I don't know their names. I'll do anything necessary to remember a name because a name represents a person's being, his identity, even his worth. My ability to recall that name is necessary in the development of a meaningful relationship. If I forget a name, I will apologize and ask the person to remind me. I write down names I want to remember. I ask others the names of people I want to address.

Many Bible study groups and churches provide name tags for their members. This is an excellent idea. Name tags should be made available to every person in that group or congregation. And they should be worn on the right side of the coat or dress, not the left. That way I can read the name when we shake hands without diverting my eyes to the left and revealing my need to be reminded.

Many groups provide get-acquainted times for their members. Those occasions are invaluable. One church service included a get-acquainted time with a novel twist. "Let's have a New Testament get-acquainted time this morning," the pastor said. "We will only use first names—no last names are allowed." I liked that. We were forced to limit our interest solely to the individual, not to his family or his business.

2. Talking with people means listening. I wear a hearing aid and I'm soon to be fitted for a second one. I feel no shame or embarrassment about wearing hearing aids. From the moment I placed that first little unit in my right ear I've sensed only sheer delight. I want one in each ear because I want to hear what people are saying. If I can't hear what is being said, a meaningful relationship is impossible. Listening is imperative for oneness.

Furthermore, I won't allow myself to be distracted when I'm listening to someone. I'll turn off the television or the radio when someone is talking to me because I want to hear everything that is being said to me. If I don't hear what is being said, I will ask for it to be repeated. If I can't hear fully with my ears, I will do my best to read a person's lips. There can be no talking *with* people without listening. Being a good listener is essential to a meaningful relationship.

3. Talking with people means asking questions. Questions which build meaningful relationships begin with those that are totally nonthreatening, like "Where do you work?" or "Where do you live?" Your questions should progress slowly to deeper levels until the conversation is redirected to spiritual issues, like "Where do you attend church?" or "When did you receive Christ into your life?"

Most small group Bible studies include insightful questions that are designed to open up people to one another. An excellent resource for such material is the *Serendipity Training Manual for Groups* by Lyman Coleman. Another book that is filled with questions and group games designed to help people get acquainted is *The Serendipity Youth Ministry Encyclopedia* edited by Lyman Coleman and available from Serendipity House, Box 1012, Littleton, CO 80160.

Meaningful relationships develop slowly. The questions that enable us to know one another must be spaced in such a way that our new friends feel comfortable in responding. The answers they give provide opportunities for us to identify needs and respond with insights which may be helpful in their lives.

8

Laying Yourself Wide Open

❦

Meaningful relationships are characterized by vulnerability.

The willingness to allow oneself to be criticized, hurt, wounded, or even destroyed for the sake of another is called vulnerability. Jesus is the ultimate example of vulnerability. He stripped Himself of all the protective garments of Deity, exposed Himself to humanity, and then even permitted humanity to slay Him—all for the sake of humanity.

Vulnerability requires me to lower my defenses, remove my mask, open myself to others, and then allow others to open themselves to me.

Letting the Inside Out

My major depression was the most humiliating experience of my life. To spend 16 weeks in the psychiatric ward of Veteran's Hospital was, I thought, the end of my career as a pastor. For years afterward I refused to talk about it. I refused to acknowledge my illness as depression. I refused to become vulnerable about the issue.

Eight years after my release and reentry into ministry, I felt constrained to go public about my depression. The site was a popular Bible conference center where I was the guest speaker for the week. On Thursday night I told my story. I painfully described my unpredictable mood swings, my uncontrolled anger, my ambivalence, my sense of failure, my desire to withdraw, my emptiness, my aloneness, and my thoughts of suicide.

I described my admission to Ward 7E. I verbalized my feelings as I walked through those double steel doors, was searched and showered, and then deprived of my clothing. I tried to describe the feelings of rejection I sensed in the withdrawal of the Christian community and the distrust of some of my closest friends.

I took my audience as far down into my black hole of my depression as I could take them with my verbal description. I wanted them to feel what I felt. I wanted them to understand depression and be sympathetic to those who suffer from it. I wanted them to realize that even Christians can experience it.

Then I brought them up out of my black hole by explaining to them that my depression was only temporary. I wanted them to hear the miracle of my recovery. I wanted to tell them about a sovereign God who supernaturally lifted me from my deep depression and returned me to His service. I wanted to show them that what God did with the depressions of Moses, Elijah, Paul, Peter, and Jonah, He can still do today.

When I was finished I felt naked. I wanted to run and hide. Instead I experienced a new kinship with struggling humanity. A prominent pastor and his wife waited until everyone was gone. The wife buried her head on my shoulder and wept. "Don Baker, you have told my story," she said. She explained that she had been hospitalized a number of times for depression during their early ministry, but she had told no one for fear of hurting her husband's ministry.

Two years later my counselor, Emery Nester, and I published the book *Depression*. Since then thousands of people have written to express their gratitude for the help our book has been to them. But it cost me something. It cost Martha and me the pain that always accompanies vulnerability. It cost us the confidence of church members who were searching for reasons to distrust us. It cost us some friends—not many—who withdrew in their discomfort with my disclosure. But the cost was insignificant in comparison to the benefits reaped in the lives of others who were helped through my story.

Recently, after 15 years, I revisited Ward 7E. As I punched the elevator button to the seventh floor, I wondered how I would handle seeing the place again. The lobby looked the same. The walls were the same color. The double doors were still in place. The long corridor was still wide and foreboding.

The head psychiatrist met me at the door and asked if he could be of help. "No thanks," I said. "I'm just a former inmate recalling some vivid and unhappy memories."

As we talked he asked me my name. I told him. "Are you the one who wrote the book on depression?" he asked. I nodded. "Thank you, thank you, thank you," he said enthusiastically. "It's so seldom that anyone who has been seriously depressed can put the feelings of depression into words. Your book has been invaluable to us."

It costs something to become vulnerable, but it rewards us daily as people claim to be helped from it. I no longer resist revealing my humanness. It enables others to admit their problems. Vulnerability gives others hope and constantly opens them to seek help.

Vulnerability, genuine empathy, and nonpossessive warmth are character traits which are usually developed in the furnace of pain. But when our sovereign Lord allows us to endure these painful experiences, we can use them as tools for establishing meaningful relationships.

Take a Look Inside

Vulnerability requires constant self-examination. It's impossible to open yourself to others if you are unwilling to look at yourself honestly and critically. And sometimes the best way to examine yourself is to ask others what they see in you.

Twice each year my staff and I left the city and met together for a two- or three-day retreat. Our agenda was usually full. But regardless of the heavy thinking and planning that confronted us, the first day was always devoted to the ritual of evaluation.

I began with the question, "How are we doing?" My second question was, "Have I offended anyone?" Rather than throw the question to the group, I addressed it to each individual, usually expanding it in order to make it more personal. I asked Dick Wahlstrom, our counselor, "Is there any distance between us? Have I said anything that troubled you?"

I asked our minister of music, "Frank, do you still feel comfortable on the platform with me? Have I made too many demands of you?"

I often asked a new staff person, "Do I intimidate you?" Sometimes they answered yes, and when they did others often acknowledged similar feelings in their relationship to me. We then proceeded to disarm negative feelings by addressing them.

Often I asked, "How were the sermons last Sunday? Was the truth clearly taught? Was the application personally relevant? Was the message portable?"

Many times the answer was no. Negative responses like that were threatening to us until we learned to work through them and walk away with positive suggestions for improvement.

Meaningful relationships need the vulnerability of self-examination, constructive criticism, and positive correction. In the Book of Acts such mutual evaluation was constant. At the conclusion of each missionary journey, the apostle Paul delivered an extensive report to the congregation for their consideration and approval (Acts 14:26-28).

No relationship can be expected to remain in good health continually. There are times when corrective action must be taken. One of my coworkers was so insecure that I was relieved when he left. Another fell into sin and had to be lovingly disciplined and restored. A third had to be corrected when he failed to maintain a group consciousness and allowed his individualism to reign.

Relationships require periodic evaluation and correction from within and without. But corrective action can never be implemented successfully when arrogance or pride keeps us from the vulnerability of confessing our weakness and admitting our need for help.

Taking Off Our Armor

Meaningful relationships are intended to be disarming. Such relationships should help us take off the defensive armor which often keeps us from the oneness Christ prayed for.

People are seldom separated by principles or external issues. The problems are usually internal and personal.

One common problem is a poor self-image. Feelings of inferiority and low self-esteem can disrupt relationships. If I don't like me, I probably won't like you. In his book *Healing for Damaged Relationships*,

David Seamands says: "Low self-esteem is one of Satan's most powerful weapons. It destroys our dreams, it limits our potential, and it damages our relationships."[1]

Feelings of inferiority and inadequacy are the enemies of meaningful relationships. But strangely enough, feelings of inferiority and inadequacy can also be overcome in a meaningful relationship when we drop our shields and let others minister to us.

My feelings of inferiority made it difficult for me to establish meaningful relationships. My first step to a healthy self-image was taken a few days after a group session where self-image was the subject of discussion. I asked a man whom I greatly admired, and to whom I felt terribly inferior, what he thought of me. I expected only insults. Instead his honest reply was, "Don Baker, you're the most all-together man I've ever met. I'd give anything to be like you." I was stunned. I always wanted to be like him. I never dreamed he wanted to be like me. My frightening moment of vulnerability was transformed into an experience of positive relationship building.

In the years since then I've learned that 95 percent of us suffer from the same problem: the limiting feelings of inferiority. These feelings cause us to fear the risks of self-disclosure, one of which is rejection. When I was finally able to explore my feelings of inferiority and verbalize them to someone I could trust, I realized that my fears were nearly universal and that they could be overcome.

One choir director I know was frightfully insecure. He had grown up in a legalistic family where his father was too strict and demanding. The lingering wound he carried was perfectionism which caused him to place unrealistic demands upon himself and produced a threatened response to any criticism.

One of his choir members said to him one day, "We didn't do very well Sunday did we?"

The director retorted brusquely, "What do you mean? I thought it was all right."

The member's observation was correct. In fact, he was being very kind because the choir number was lousy. But the defensive director felt threatened and took the comment as personal criticism. His hostile response was like a shield raised to protect himself.

The wise choir member got up from his chair, walked over to the choir leader, put an arm around his shoulders, and said, "Hey, I'm your friend, remember?" They both relaxed.

A relationship has come a long way when potential destruction can be defused that easily.

To the insecure, even constructive criticism is at best difficult to receive. "What happened to the steak tonight?" When a wife hears that question at the supper table, she knows the steak isn't what she wanted it to be. She knows exactly what's wrong with it. But she responds defensively, "What do you mean, 'What happened to the steak tonight?' Can't I do anything to please you?"

The issue is not really the meat. It's probably her deep insecurity or a long string of unresolved conflicts. She's protecting herself instead of becoming vulnerable and resolving the issue.

We were guests in a home where the husband asked, "What happened to the meat?" His wife's response was surprising and delightful: "It's awful isn't it? The phone rang, and I got to talking and forgot to check my timer." We all relaxed.

When we take off our defensive armor and become vulnerable to each other, meaningful relationships will result.

Laying Down Our Weapons

The vulnerability which characterizes meaningful relationships not only requires us to take off our defensive armor but also to lay down the offensive weapons which block oneness.

Bitterness is a weapon which can disrupt relationships. When I found myself struggling to stay productive at age 44, I allowed bitterness to sift down into my soul and harden like concrete. My bitterness was really directed toward God, but since I thought it was disrespectful to level my bitterness at Him, I unleashed my bitterness toward the people I loved most—with frightening consequences. I was only able to acknowledge and deal with my feelings when I opened myself to a friend who helped me explore my soul and understand what we found there.

Self-centered pride is destructive to relationships. Pride won't listen to other people. If it does it only allows another person's problem to elevate its own ego.

Vengeance is a destructive weapon in relationships. Jesus modeled the exact opposite of vengeance by refusing to retaliate against those who persecuted Him and eventually killed Him. The word "long-suffering" appropriately describes His response. We are also admonished to lay down our tendency toward revenge and build oneness through long-suffering.

Anger is a weapon which blocks meaningful relationships. I learned the value of disarming anger in relationships during one of my group therapy sessions in the psychiatric ward.

There were nine of us in my group—blacks, whites, and Hispanics. Most were young casualties from the Vietnam War. Few if any had any relationship to the church. I was twice their age and a Baptist preacher.

I had some problems with my group. The language was obscene and vulgar. I disliked the therapist. I couldn't quit, but I could remain silent—and I did. Each day the counselor would ask, "Do you have anything to talk about, Mr. Baker?" And each day I'd shake my head in silence.

During one session I became frightfully angry at the direction the group was taking. I seethed in silence until I could contain my anger no longer. It erupted in rage. The others, seemingly unruffled by my outburst, turned their attention to me and listened attentively to my charges and accusations.

When I finished, a young Hispanic said, "Hey, he *can* talk after all." They then stood as a group, smiled approvingly at me, and applauded.

I was ashamed of my outburst and embarrassed by my statements, but I was totally bewildered by their response. I did not feel disapproval. I did not sense rejection. No one argued with me or defended himself against my attack. They seemed genuinely pleased with what I'd done.

The counselor then complimented me. "That was good," he said. "I was afraid you were never going to accept us. But I have one question: Why don't you raise your questions and level your charges before you get angry? Don't you think maybe you waited too long?"

A profound self-realization exploded in my brain. As a Christian I had always viewed anger as sin. I would suppress it, control it, hide it, and disguise it. I'd do anything to keep from displaying it. But it would eventually erupt in rage.

In the safety of a group of men who had little in common beyond their personal need, I learned a lesson that changed my life. Anger defensively repressed leads to an explosion which can seriously damage relationships. But angry feelings which are exposed through a posture of vulnerability can build meaning-ful relationships.

In one of our small groups, one apprehensive member exclaimed, "I don't think I like this. I really don't want to be here." He expected immediate rejec-tion.

But instead someone asked, "Would you care to tell us why?" He did. He explored his feelings as he explained them and then he relaxed. And the group was closer because of it.

So many of us feel that if we could just eliminate these internal human weaknesses and problems we would probably experience meaningful relationships. I think just the opposite is true. If we could just take off our armor, lay down our weapons, and establish meaningful relationships, we could probably elimi-nate our human weaknesses.

Dr. James C. Dobson provides a tragic example of this in a story recorded in his book, *Hide & Seek*.

> A young man began his childhood with all the classic handicaps and disadvantages. His mother was a powerfully built, dominating woman who found it diffiult to love anyone. She had been married three times, and her second husband divorced her because she beat him up regularly. The father of the child I'm describing was her third husband; he died of a heart attack a few months before the child's birth. As a consequence, the mother had to work long hours from his earliest childhood.
>
> She gave him no affection, no love, no discipline and no training during those early years. She even forbade him to call her at work. Other children had little to do with him, so he was alone most of the time. He was absolutely rejected from his earliest childhood. He was

ugly and poor and untrained and unlovable. When the man was 13 years old, a school psychologist commented that he probably didn't know the meaning of the word "love." During adolescence, the girls would have nothing to do with him and he fought with the boys.

Despite a high IQ, he failed academically, and finally dropped out during his third year of high school. He thought he might find a new acceptance in the Marine Corps; they reportedly built men, and he wanted to be one. But his problems went with him. The other Marines laughed at him and ridiculed him. He fought back, resisted authority, and was court-martialed and thrown out of the Marines with an undesirable discharge. So there he was, a young man in his early twenties, absolutely friendless and shipwrecked. He was small and scrawny in stature. He had an adolescent squeak in his voice. He was balding. He had no talent, no skill, no sense of worthiness. He didn't even have a driver's license.

Once again he thought he could run from his problems so he went to live in a foreign country. But he was rejected there too. Nothing had changed. While there, he married a girl who herself had been an illegitimate child and brought her back to America with him. Soon, she began to develop the same contempt for him that everyone else displayed. She bore him two children, but he never enjoyed the status and respect that a father should have. His marriage continued to crumble. His wife demanded more and more things that he could not provide. Instead of being his ally against the bitter world, as he hoped, she became his most vicious opponent. She could outfight him, and she learned to bully him. On one occasion, she locked him in the bathroom as punishment. Finally she forced him to leave.

He tried to make it on his own, but he was terribly lonely. After days of solitude, he went home and literally begged her to take him back. He surrendered all pride. He crawled. He accepted humiliation. He came on her terms. Despite his meager salary, he brought her seventy-eight dollars as a gift, asking her to take it and spend it any way she wished. But she laughed at him. She belittled his feeble attempts to supply the family's needs. She ridiculed his failure. She made fun of his sexual impotency in front of a friend who was there. At one point, he fell on his knees and wept bitterly, as the greater darkness of his private nightmare enveloped him.

Finally, in silence, he pleaded no more. No one wanted him. No one ever wanted him. He was perhaps the most rejected man of our time. His ego lay shattered in a fragmented dust!

The next day, he was a strangely different man. He arose, went to the garage and took down a rifle he had hidden there. He carried it with him to his newly-acquired job at the book storage building. And from a window on the sixth floor of that building, shortly after noon, November 22, 1963, he sent two bullets crashing into the head of President John Fitzgerald Kennedy.

Feelings of inferiority and inadequacy are the enemies of meaningful relationships, but strangely enough, feelings of inferiority and inadequacy can only be overcome in a meaningful relationship.

9

Reach Out and Touch Someone

❦

Meaningful relationships are marked by sharing and caring.

Bearing each other's burdens through sharing and caring is wonderfully biblical (Galatians 6:2). The early Christians in the Book of Acts modeled this trait: "They began selling their property and possessions, and were sharing them with all, as anyone might have need. . . . Not one of them claimed that anything belonging to him was his own: but all things were common property to them" (Acts 2:45; 4:32).

It's difficult to find a modern-day illustration of these verses. Social and civil agencies have taken over our welfare programs. Whatever sharing and caring is done by the church is usually only a token ministry. But I discovered a remarkable instance of biblical sharing and caring several years ago near the city of Cottage Grove, Oregon.

In the early 1980s the unemployment situation in our country was severe. NBC news reported a 34 percent national unemployment rate. In Cottage Grove, near the heart of Oregon's depressed timber industry, it was even higher—an astronomical 44 percent. Several saw mills had closed. Thousands were out of work. The recession had reached the depression stage.

Fourteen miles out of Cottage Grove, up a winding road past Dorena Lake, lies the little town of Culp Creek. When the Bohemia Mill closed down, virtually the entire population of Culp Creek was unemployed. In the little Community Church of Culp Creek, a large percentage of the members were dependent on Bohemia Mill for their income. When the mill closed and the recession reached its lowest ebb, the members' concern was not for the survival of the corporate church but for the welfare of its member families.

Rev. Parry Koosshian told me how the little congregation faced the crisis. The Community Church of Culp Creek began to practice biblical oneness through caring and sharing. The members of the congregation who were working actually endorsed their paychecks over to the church and the church dispersed the money among all its members until Bohemia Mill resumed operations.

Of course all Christians are not required to do what the early church and the Community Church of Culp Creek did. But oneness in relationships is always strengthened when individuals sacrifice to meet the material needs of others.

Sharing Beyond Our Circle

A Buddhist Vietnamese family moved in across the street from a church I was pastoring and opened a French bakery. Wanting to express the love of Christ to this family, our church did everything we could to help them, even to taking a significant offering to keep them in business. But when an arsonist set fire to their building they were forced to give up their business and their home.

But our caring had just begun. We immediately moved the entire family of six into a house that was equipped for such an emergency. We supplied the house with furniture, filled the refrigerator, clothed the children, and provided for necessities.

The Buddhist family was so overwhelmed that they all became Christians. The mother told me later, "In Vietnam I was told to find Christ, but I couldn't find Him anywhere. In Cambodia I was told to find Christ, but I couldn't find Him there either. In a crowded refugee boat I was told to find Christ, but I couldn't find Him on the ocean. In America I was told to find Christ, and I found Him—right here in your people."

Christians are certainly committed to taking care of the needs of their own. But they must also reach outside their group and minister to the world around them in caring ways. Sharing and caring is part of our very life. As James so pointedly asked: "If a brother or sister is without clothing and in need of daily food, and one of you says to them, 'Go in peace, be warmed and be filled,' and yet you do not give them what is necessary for their body, what use is that?" (James 2:15,16).

More than the Material

A meaningful relationship shares more than monetary and material resources. Biblical caring includes sharing possessions and resources that are often more valuable than material goods: time, energy, wisdom, love, compassion, and encouragement.

When I was struggling in my black hole of depression years ago, a friend gave me, not money, but his time, his compassion, and his wisdom. During that bleak period in my life I would preach on Sundays and then withdraw from my people—even from my family—attempting to find solace in silence. I didn't want to talk to anyone or see anyone. I wanted to be alone. At times I even wanted to die.

Emery Nester chopped away at my wall of isolation until it eventually crumbled. Every day for eight days he called me. And every day for eight days I rejected him.

"Hi Don, this is Emery," he would say.

"Hi Emery," I would answer in a flat, impatient sort of way.

"How are you today?"

"Fine."

"Can I be of any help to you?"

"No thanks."

"Can I take you out to lunch?"

"Nope."

"Well, I just wanted to let you know that I love you and that I'm praying for you."

"Thanks Emery."

After a very unfriendly good-bye, I would replace the receiver and retreat again into my silence.

On the eighth day my resistance finally wore down. I accepted his invitation and met him at a local restaurant. His spirit was as full of love as mine was of hostility. I wanted to run. I wanted to hide. I wanted to hurt this man who had dared to pluck me from my self-imposed prison.

When he mentioned the word "depression" I was angry. I didn't want to talk about it or even think about it. Then he surprised me by saying, "I'm just coming out of a depression myself." Suddenly I softened.

"Let me tell you a story," he continued. "A man was lost in the wilderness and he came upon a stranger. He said to the stranger, 'I'm lost. Can you show me the way out of this wilderness?' The stranger said to him, 'No, I cannot show you the way out of the wilderness, but I can walk *with you* in your wilderness.'"

I crumbled. My resistance was broken. From that day on, Emery Nester, a professional counselor and friend, walked with me through my personal wilderness. He gave me 100 hours of his time, his wisdom, his energy, his compassion, and his love. He and his wife Mary Ann gave me their sacred evenings. Not once was I made to feel like an intruder. Not once did I sense impatience or rejection in them. I was in such a fragile state that, if I had detected the slightest clue that they felt imposed upon, I would have never returned.

Thanks to the selfless sharing and caring of Emery and Mary Ann Nester, I was able to walk out of my wilderness. Since then, following their example, I have been able to guide countless others out of the wilderness of depression.

Caring Without Strings

Building meaningful relationships through caring and sharing requires that we love others nonpossessively. As parents it was difficult for Martha and me to let our children go as they grew into adulthood. I've read many books and articles on the empty nest syndrome, but none quite prepared me for the moment the children left us. We had to learn to love them without possessing them.

Meaningful relationships learn to care and share through what has been called nonpossessive warmth. Nonpossessive warmth means I love you but would never take advantage of you.

Nonpossessive warmth means I'll give to you but never demand anything in return.

Nonpossessive warmth will even allow another to fail. Jesus displayed this trait when He predicted Peter's denial but did not prevent it from happening.

It was hard for me to allow my children to make

mistakes. I wanted so much to make them do the right thing. It is hard for me to allow a friend to proceed with what I think is a foolish idea. I want so much to make his decisions for him.

But nonpossessive warmth permits failure.

Nonpossessive warmth allows one to grow at his own pace, not at the pace I feel he should grow.

Nonpossessive warmth allows one to be what he believes God wants him to be.

Nonpossessive warmth will let go when letting go is what is wanted or needed. Jesus let go of Judas even though it meant His death. He released all His disciples to flee from Him in cowardice and never rebuked them for it. He gave of His days, His nights, His wisdom, His energy, and ultimately His life—and asked for nothing in return.

Nonpossessive warmth means I love you but I won't fight you, I'll serve you but I won't use you, I'll show you but I won't manipulate you.

Nonpossessive love means I love you with no strings attached and I'll continue to love you even if you stop loving me.

Caring with Feeling

It was along the western shore of Galilee on one of His busiest days, while surrounded by a multitude of people, that Jesus sensed a special need nearby. It was a woman who had been hemorrhaging for 12 years. Doctors were unable to help her. But she was certain that if she could just touch the robe of Jesus she'd be healed. She touched His robe and she was healed (Mark 5:25-29).

"And immediately Jesus, perceiving in Himself that the power proceeding from Him had gone forth, turned around in the crowd and said, 'Who touched My garments?' " (Mark 5:30). Jesus' perception was keen. He not only *knew* people and their needs, He also *felt* them.

Developing meaningful relationships through caring and sharing means that we must learn to read people and sense their needs. We must listen to what people say, to be sure. But we must also learn to read their body language, their eyes, and if possible even their minds. Often what people say is far different from what they mean.

I'm not talking about being psychic. I'm talking about being empathetic. Empathy is the projection of one's own consciousness into another person's being. It's understanding what someone else is going through and feeling with them what they are feeling. Empathy seeks to read people in order to know when they are agreeing or disagreeing, pleading for help or seeking privacy, relaxed or impatient, comfortable or uncomfortable, weary or refreshed, angry or fearful or hurting.

These are things we need to know about people in order to care for them. But people don't always feel free to tell us about their inner struggles. We need to learn to read them through nonverbal signals. When we detect any of these problems, and they're confirmed, then we're free to move in and share that pain.

Empathy is more than sympathy. Empathy is the ability to properly discern a need and move in the direction of that need to the point where we actually share the pain. Empathy is learning to "rejoice with those who rejoice, and weep with those who weep" (Romans 12:15).

A couple recently reminded me of my first encounter with them. They had just lost their firstborn in childbirth. I was asked by one of my church members to call on them. They were strangers to me at the time.

"We were alone in the hospital room," they recounted the story for me, "when our own pastor came in. He sat down, looked at us, and asked, 'What sin is God punishing you for?' We were speechless with shock at his question.

"At that moment you came in, Pastor Baker. You were unaware of the question our pastor had just asked us. You introduced yourself, sat down, and said, 'I'm sorry you've lost your baby, but I do know how you feel.'

"That made us a little angry until you added, 'We lost our little baby too.' We immediately realized that you *did* know just how we felt.

"You went to the cemetery with us, conducted a little graveside service for us, and then showed us your baby's grave. You helped us see beyond our sorrow until we were finally able to ask, 'When should we have another baby?'

" 'As soon as the doctor says it's all right,' you answered."

After telling me the story I had forgotten, the couple introduced me to the "baby" who was born after they lost their firstborn. Their child was now the wife of a pastoral staff member and a mother herself.

The couple again expressed their gratitude by saying, "Thank you for entering into our sorrow with us." That's genuine empathy.

10

A Shelter from the Storm

❦

A meaningful relationship is a place of safety and peace.

It's the characteristic which Julie alluded to when she told me on the airplane about her ideal church. She said she wanted to be involved in a church where she felt

> free to fail,
> free to succeed,
> free to weep,
> free to rejoice, and
> free to be different.

The disciples failed—all of them (Mark 14:50). How many of us would have turned away from them for their cowardice on the night of Jesus' betrayal? We probably would have excommunicated Peter for his denial (Mark 14:66-72). Yet each experienced the grace of forgiveness and each went on to become essential to the advancement of God's kingdom throughout the earth.

An 86-year-old Christian once boastfully said to me, "I have never sinned, I have never cried, and I have never said I'm sorry." It was not the appropriate time or place for me to explore his statements with him. But I allowed myself to feel the pain that comes from hearing such a pronouncement. He might just as well have said, "I have never lived."

This poor man was not free to be himself because he did not feel secure in his relationship with God, with his family, or with his church. He couldn't just relax, express his humanness, and enjoy his relationships. He was always afraid he would make a mistake and be rejected. He felt he had to be perfect—or at least act perfect—in order to be accepted. He would never survive in a meaningful relationship—in fact, he would never admit he needed one.

Safety in Numbers

This man is representative of a great number of Christians who never link up with anyone in meaningful relationship. They are stoic, fearful islands of humanity who manage to remain separated from others by the vast distance of their dishonesty. They can never admit to having a need. They can never enjoy the satisfaction that comes from another person's help. They can never know the peace that comes with forgiveness.

They hide their mistakes, they mask their feelings, they reject their limitations. They sit high on their walls of indifference sneering at struggling humanity. Ultimately they fall and break into a pile of Humpty Dumpty-like pieces that can never be put back together again.

I was once like that. I found it hard to say I don't know. I found it even harder to say I'm sorry. I found it easier to feign illness than to admit incompetence. I found it even easier to place blame elsewhere than to accept it myself.

Early in my ministry I served as associate pastor to Dr. William Kerr at Hinson Church in Portland. In his absence one Sunday I was to serve communion.

The communion has always been a big thing at Hinson: a thousand worshipers, a couple of dozen deacons, high stacks of trays holding the bread and the juice.

All went well until I began distributing the bread. The bread plates were separated by paper doilies. I was to take one bread plate at a time, pass it to the deacon chairman to my right, and slip the doily onto a shelf under the table. But instead I lifted the first plate from the stack, placed it on the shelf under the table, and passed the doily to the deacon. I returned to the stack for the second plate, slipped it onto the shelf, and again passed the doily to the deacon.

The deacon chairman never moved. He let me keep piling doilies in his hands until I realized what I was doing. Then with great dignity and not even a hint of a problem, he allowed me to retrieve the doilies from him and correct my mistake.

I was humiliated. I sought for excuses that refused to come. I considered flight—far and fast. At the close of the service, one of the deacons met me at the door and said, "The deacons wish to see you in the board room."

When I walked into the board room I was certain that my public ministry was finished. The deacons were all seated in a circle and silent. No one looked at me. No one spoke to me. I sat down nervously and awaited the inevitable.

As if on cue they all began to laugh. Their laughter lifted higher and higher until it finally lifted me out of myself and I was laughing with them. Then without a single word being spoken, they all got up and left.

Some months afterward a number of pastors were having lunch together. One of them asked each man in attendance, "What was the most significant spiritual experience in your life this past year?" Each one responded with a profound answer.

When my turn came I said, "The most significant spiritual experience in my life this past year was the Sunday I learned to laugh at myself." My response was strange to most of them. But for me, laughing with the deacons was a red-letter day in my life.

Developing a working relationship with a staff has never been easy for me. Before going to Hinson Church as senior pastor in 1974 I had never in my ministry attended a staff meeting. At Hinson, molding a large staff was a necessity. But I didn't know how to do it so I avoided it.

Often on staff meeting day I would call in sick. I'd ask my associate Dick Wahlstrom to take over for me. I retreated into my fear and shame until I could stand it no longer. Then I went in late and pretended to know what I was doing.

One day I finally admitted the obvious to my staff. I said, "I really don't know what to do in these meetings. I don't know whether to address problems, grapple with your needs, teach the Scriptures to you, or spend this time in prayer. Please help me."

It was at that moment that we began to experience safety with each other. We learned to laugh together, cry together, agree, and disagree. The only thing we couldn't do was hide from each other. We learned the great lesson of being human in front of each other, admitting to our limitations, and accepting one another.

It's seldom that Christians are honored with such an experience of safety in a relationship. But that is what God intended to happen in a community of Christians. None of the initial leaders, Peter and Paul included, was a spiritual superman. They were just men who acknowledged their limitations to God and to each other, and then drew strength from God and from each other.

One of the priceless moments of oneness on our Hinson staff occurred when a staff member began to cry during a meeting. "Please pray for me," he said, sobbing. "I really don't think I have what's needed for this job and I don't want to fail." Because of his willingness to trust himself to the group, he didn't fail. Instead his confession of need that morning was his first step toward success.

I've spent time with AIDS patients in a hospice in Long Beach, California. Their condition is pitiful. Their future is hopeless, but they're so refreshing to talk to. They have nothing left to hide. Their openness, their transparency, and their honesty are delightful. If we could relate to each other with that kind of simple trust our relationships would be more meaningful.

Have you ever noticed how transparent Jesus was? His disciples asked to see where He lived. His answer was, "Come, and you will see" (John 1:39). He openly spoke of His limitations. He was thirsty (John 19:28) and tired (Hebrews 4:15). He wept (John 11:35) and was troubled (John 12:27). He didn't want to die (Matthew 26:39).

Jesus drew close to humanity by becoming one of us. We draw close to each other in the same way. When are we going to admit to one another that we have problems and need help? The Christian community begins to display meaningful relationships when we allow ourselves the privilege of being ourselves and then allow others to strengthen our weaknesses.

Peace Among the People

A meaningful relationship is a place of peace. The apostle Paul calls it "the unity of the Spirit in the bond of peace" (Ephesians 4:3).

I often speak in churches on the subject of relationships. My goal is to begin moving people in the direction of meaningful relationships. I discuss subjects like fractured relationships and how to deal with them, unresolved inner conflicts that destroy relationships, the causes and solutions for floating anger, how to control the urge to get even, and how to live with people you don't like.

An interesting phenomenon takes place as I lead groups through a week of teaching on relationships. The spirit in the participants moves from aloneness and alienation toward oneness. It begins to feel good. The individuals who continue to attend all the sessions gain insights, seek and receive forgiveness, and begin to recognize the common threads that pass through all of us.

At the close of the conference I ask everyone to stand. Then I invite them to join hands, but first I offer this explanation: "There may be some here tonight who for some reason really don't want to hold hands with the persons standing beside you. It may be a cultural thing or a personal thing. It may be that you don't want to get your hands dirty. You may fear contracting AIDS. You may have arthritis or an injury and holding hands hurts. We want you to feel free not to hold hands. We will not be critical of you or withdraw from you. We will not judge you."

Some people opt not to, but most people join hands. Then I say to them, "Many of you are holding the hand of a friend or a family member. You don't feel awkward about that. But some of you are holding hands with a stranger—possibly someone of the opposite sex. That's always a little clumsy."

I then ask them, "Have you ever noticed that, when holding a stranger's hand, we're careful never to move the slightest muscle? We're afraid to even twitch. We don't want to send the wrong message."

The feeling of relief and relaxation in the group following my statement is universal. The smiles are there. The warmth is there. Then I tell them, "Now don't squeeze too hard because it just might hurt. But squeeze just a little. Let them know you're there. Say to them with just a slight squeeze that you love them. It's all right because you do love them and they love you. And it's okay to tell them in this way."

The group relaxes even more, and many of them, for the first time, look into the faces and deep into the eyes of the ones standing beside them.

Then we sing, "Bind us together, Lord, bind us together with cords that cannot be broken." That little prayer chorus is beautifully reflective of the concern of every heart. When we're finished singing, most of the hostility has seeped away. Most of our alienation has given place to peace. Most of our loneliness has relaxed in the presence of oneness. It's an indescribable peace.

I tell them, "This is a taste of what peace is like. It will get even better, but this is what we're after and what we want to preserve in our relationships. Don't let anything take it from you. If you haven't found it in your relationships, seek it at all costs."

Meaningful relationships provide us with a place of peace.

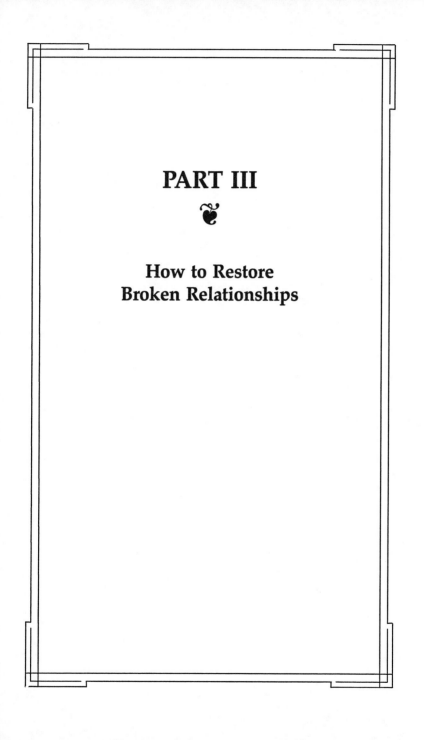

PART III

❦

How to Restore
Broken Relationships

11

There's Hope for Broken Relationships

❦

Broken relationships can be restored.

Broken relationships must be restored.

There is no alternative to reconciliation. When fractures occur, we have no other options. We are commanded to seek healing.

Jesus addresses the problem of broken relationships twice. Once in Matthew 5 and again in Matthew 18.

In the first, He addresses us as the ones guilty of offending another. He says,

> If therefore you are presenting your offering at the altar, and there remember that your brother has something against you, leave your offering there before the altar, and go your way; first be reconciled to your brother, and then come and present your offering (Matthew 5:23,24).

In the second, He addresses us as the ones who have been offended. He says,

> And if your brother sins, go and reprove him in private; if he listens to you, you have won your brother (Matthew 18:15).

In each instance the goal is the same—to seek reconciliation.

In each verse the command is the same—"Go."

The word "Go" means to take the initiative.

It means to confront the person.

It means to question.

It means to probe.

It means to search out the problem and then correct it, regardless of who's to blame.

Broken Relationships Can Be Restored

Let me tell you a story.

The spring day was crystalline clear in the Columbia basin—one of those rare days when not the slightest hint of a cloud marred the endless blue that stretched as far as the eye could see. In the distance the snow-laden peak of majestic Mt. Hood lifted its head high above the world. It stood as a sentinel, standing perpetual guard over the lush green hills and valleys of the Oregon country.

The Columbia River appeared as a band of shining silver as it continued its uninterrupted flow from the distant Canadian Athabasca glacier down to the shores of the mighty Pacific Ocean. The brilliant multicolored sails of dozens of little wind-surfers could be seen in the distance. A tug, pushing a heavy barge laden with oil, struggled against the rushing current to move its cargo upriver to the Tri-Cities of southeastern Washington.

Only the occasional whine of a passenger jet on its descent to the Portland International Airport interrupted the silence of a beautiful day.

Henry walked carefully among the trees he had planted as a youth and nurtured with care through the many years that his 120-acre apple ranch had provided a comfortable living for him and his wife Trina.

He examined each tree, looking for any hint of apple maggots or blight or insects that could spoil or mar his annual crop. He stood back and marveled as he did every year, at the countless morsels of fruit that hung down from the branches like brightly colored ornaments on a Christmas tree.

Suddenly he heard a distant voice, tiny, high-pitched, but insistent. His heart leaped as a happy word formed in his ears.

"Grampa—Grampa."

The little voice squealed with expectancy and then almost scolded with impatience as it received no answer.

Henry bent down to see beneath the low-hanging branches that obscured his vision. Then he saw her—whirling in all directions—searching for the grandfather she was unable to find.

"Tracy," he called.

He watched as the little three-year-old bundle of joy turned and finally spotted him. There were very few things in Henry's life that gave him as much happiness as his daughter's little girl.

She was boundless energy,
   perpetual motion,
      insistent chatter,
         insatiable curiosity, and
            innocent love—
all wrapped up in a perfect little package.

She smelled like sweet perfume, felt like the softness of a fluffy white cloud, and spoke with a wisdom far above her years.

She looked through soft blue eyes that seemed to penetrate all the walls that adults spend a lifetime building.

She laughed with an insistent little giggle that made any solemnity virtually impossible.

She hugged—only seldom—but when she did, those little arms warmed her grampa to the very distant reaches of his soul.

Whenever her stubby little fingers touched his, his big, calloused hand would wrap around hers and caress it as if it were earth's most priceless jewel.

And when she'd finally slow down, reach out her tired arms, and ask him to hold her, his world would stop—whatever he was doing could wait—and he would tenderly pick her up and gently hold the little one he loved so very much.

As Tracy's little legs ran across the hard, packed earth, he waited with arms outstretched, hoping that this time she might forget to play the little game that teased both of her grandparents.

She didn't.

She did again what she always did. She stopped just short of his outstretched arms and waited—and grinned and then ran—knowing that her grampa would run after her—and catch her. It was a game she loved to play.

They walked among the trees—only seldom were they side by side. She would run from one curious twig to another, pick it up, examine it, and then throw it back down again.

When he could, he would hold her up to one of the trees, let her touch a ripening apple, and then try vainly to explain in terms a three-year-old could understand, just how one of these apples would someday be turned into applesauce or even apple juice—her favorite drink.

It wasn't long before she began to reluctantly give in to her tiredness. She slowed and then stopped. Her little arms reached up and Henry lifted her off the ground and felt her head as it nestled against his neck and finally relaxed on his shoulder.

That's a relationship.

He sat on a stump and hummed "Jesus Loves Me" until her tired body went limp. Carefully he lowered Tracy's sleeping form until she was cradled in his arms.

As he studied her sleeping face, the closed eyes and the twisted curls of her light brown hair, Henry felt a strange stirring within him—a frightening sensual response to the bundle of innocence that rested against his chest.

He'd felt it before.
  He'd repressed it,
    cursed it,
      prayed about it,
        and fought to control it for most of his
        adult life.
        He'd given in to it—
a long time ago—when Tracy's mother was still quite small.

He had often wondered if she had ever remembered.

The sexual stirrings in the loins of the adoring grandfather were so inconsistent with the godliness he'd always displayed.

Henry appeared to all to be the true Christian patriarch. No one ever doubted who was the head of his household. He was rigid, demanding, and always insistent upon strict and immediate obedience. His five children knew they were loved but lived with the nagging fear of ever displeasing him.

Trina lost herself completely in her attempts to be the perfect wife and mother. She seldom expressed any wishes of her own. Her purpose in life seemed to be that of pleasing her husband and serving her children.

Each night the growing family participated in the ritual of Bible reading and prayer. Henry always read from the big family Bible that rested on the sideboard, and Henry always prayed—only Henry prayed.

To the growing children there were times when his Bible reading seemed interminable, and his prayers endless. Often they caused one or more members to be late for school or church functions in the evening. Nothing ever interfered with "devotions."

Complaints or objections were never tolerated.

He was a pillar in his church. He had served on every board and practically every committee. He had been chairman of the Building Committee and had efficiently supervised construction.

His advice was sought in everything. Everyone loved him and trusted him. He was one of those few privileged ones to move in close to the pastor and become his revered confidant.

Henry was generous to a fault—the first to give toward any worthy project and the one who usually gave the most.

But when it came to visible demonstrations of love, he was lacking. He found it impossible to hug or to touch or to kiss any of his family members, except the little ones. The deprived children found some sort of vicarious satisfaction whenever they saw their father loving their children.

Henry couldn't forgive and Henry could never forget when someone caused him the slightest displeasure. When his pastor lovingly rebuked him for being too strict with his children, Henry began setting the wheels in motion that eventually drove the church leader out of town.

Now in the orchard, on one of Oregon's beautiful spring days, those strange feelings returned—those same stirrings he'd struggled to control before began to control him. His mind began to drift in the most frightening directions. His fingers pried themselves free of Tracy's little hand and began to probe the softness of her tiny body.

Henry succumbed to the uncontrollable urgings of his flesh and did the unthinkable and the unspeakable.

He suddenly became aware of two frightened eyes searching his face. They were looking at him— through him. They were filled with fear and bewilderment. A perceptible frown creased his granddaughter's forehead.

Tracy began to squirm away from him. She finally pulled herself free and stood back and looked and studied the face of the man she had trusted so much.

Slowly she walked alongside her grandfather as they returned to the house. She was silent, unresponsive, totally disinterested in the happy world around her. Henry tried to hold her hand—she pried it free. Toby, the family dog, leaped in delight to greet them. Tracy acted as if she never saw him.

On the way home, Ellen asked her young daughter all about her trip to the orchard.

"Did you have fun with Grampa?"

"Did he show you the apples?"

"Did he lift you up to the tree?"

"Did he tell you a story?"

"Did he sing to you?"

To all these questions, her three-year-old was strangely silent. Ellen turned to see if Tracy was asleep. Tracy was snugly and safely strapped into her car seat, but she was far from asleep. Her eyes were opened wide and seemed to be peering at something—somewhere far out in space. Her face showed fear and for the first time in her short life, Ellen thought she detected the unmistakable look of shame.

Ellen dismissed her daughter's stillness and shifted her concentration back to the busy freeway that would eventually lead them home.

Tracy's quietness persisted. There was no happy greeting when her daddy came home. Instead, she ran to her room and closed the door.

"What's wrong with Tracy?" Jim asked.

"Nothing," replied Ellen. "She's been quiet all afternoon. She's probably just inventing a new game."

Jim quietly opened her bedroom door and was surprised to see his living bundle of energy curled up on the bed, knees drawn up to her chest, eyes wide open and staring, and her little thumb thrust into her mouth.

"What's the matter, honey?" he asked as he leaned over her.

Tracy was silent.

Her daddy picked up her limp body, tucked her chin into his shoulder, and asked, "Don't you feel well?"

Tracy squirmed to get even closer. Her arms gripped him more tightly than Jim could ever remember.

"Is she sick?" he asked as he carried her back into the kitchen.

"I don't think so," Ellen answered as she felt her forehead and probed her tummy.

As always, Jim and Ellen waited for Tracy to pray her little prayer of thankfulness as they sat down to eat. Instead, she was silent. When they urged her, she just shook her head from side to side.

That night after a long and worried evening, Ellen got Tracy ready for bed. She read the nighttime story, sang the nighttime lullaby, kissed her still unresponsive daughter goodnight, and started to slip out the bedroom door.

As soon as the door was closed, she heard the irresistible sobs of her little girl. She waited, but when they didn't stop, she quietly reopened the door. Tracy was standing in the corner of her bed, her favorite doll dangling from her hand, her eyes pleading for her mother's arms.

Ellen sang to Tracy, rocked her, lay down with her, threatened her—all the things parents do when children insist on staying awake. Finally she lay down again alongside her and cradled her on her arm. They both lay silent until in an unexpected moment, Tracy said, "Grampa hurt me."

"Did he, honey? I'm sure he didn't mean to."

"Grampa hurt me."

"How did Grandpa hurt you? Did you fall down?"

"Grampa hurt me."

"How, honey? Did he spank you?"

"Grampa hurt me."

Ellen sat up, looked down at her little girl, and asked again. But all she heard from quivering lips was, "Grampa hurt me."

Ellen remembered.

She had never forgotten—but she had never told anyone—not even Jim. She had borne that ugly memory that at times caused her emotions to swing like a pendulum from a murderous rage to an all-consuming guilt.

She picked up her sobbing little girl, carried her into the family room, and began to spill out to her husband her ugliest childhood memory and her adult life's greatest fear.

She was sure that her daughter had been, in some way, sexually abused by her own father.

An examination showed nothing, and Ellen's greatest fear was stilled. But both Jim and Ellen were sure that Tracy's grandfather had done something unforgivable to their little girl.

Tracy's entire personality changed. She became quiet and withdrawn and craved the protection of her parents' arms.

She played less.

She never sang.

Her chatter became little meaningless mumbles that could seldom be understood—and she never wanted to go to Grampa's house.

Jim and Ellen were furious.

They were crushed.

They were betrayed.

They were heartbroken.

Ellen poured out her anger to her mother.

Trina continued her work in the kitchen as she listened to her daughter's story. She didn't show surprise. She never expressed anger. She just listened—never denying the possibility that her husband had abused his granddaughter. When Ellen finished sobbing out her fears and her suspicions, Trina quietly took Ellen in her arms, held her close, and said, "I'm so sorry, dear."

Both Jim and Ellen leveled their anger at her dad.

"What did you do to Tracy?" they screamed.

Henry turned from his workbench in surprise, looked at his daughter in shocked disbelief, and then busied himself with his tools again.

Jim and Ellen screamed at him, argued with him, pled with him, but he remained silent.

For months the silence persisted. The distance between the two families widened. The mother always protective of her husband. The father always busy and noncommunicative. The children angry and frustrated, and a beautiful little child scarred in such a way that it seemed she'd never heal.

It was more than a year before Jim and Ellen could return to her parents' house. It was Christmas and the invitation was impossible to decline.

They tried to pretend that it was just another regular, happy, wonderful, traditional Christmastime at Grampa and Grama's house, but for one little family around the parents' table, it was nothing like it used to be.

Jim and Ellen tried to contribute to the conversation but could never find the right words to speak.

Tracy sat in quiet obedience and ate what she could—but her mind was somewhere else.

The meal went as planned, Trina was up and down, up and down, making sure that everyone had all they wanted. The atmosphere was reasonably tranquil—until Henry reached for the family Bible.

Jim's face reddened as obvious anger began to consume him. Ellen bowed her head and gripped the sides of the table and said, "Dad, please don't. . . ."

But the big family Bible found its traditional place at the head of the table. Its cover was lifted and its pages exposed. Henry thumbed through those pages until he found his place, and completely oblivious to the feelings of his children's awed disbelief, he began to read.

He continued to read until without a word, Jim lifted Tracy in his arms, pulled Ellen up from her chair, and led his family out the door into the night and back to their home.

That's a broken relationship.

Five people hungry for fellowship with one another and anxious to return to the joys they once shared.

Five people, four adults and a child, related to each other but unable to enjoy that relationship.

Five people, with the same blood, the same names, whose days and nights were spent in longing for one another, but who couldn't seek or give the love they so desperately wanted to experience.

Four adult Christians who had all experienced the forgiveness of God, but who couldn't express or find the forgiveness of men.

Finally Ellen could stand it no longer.

She missed her parents. She needed her parents. She wanted Tracy to be able to climb back up on that grandfather's knees while she was still young—but she wanted her to be able to do it without fear.

Ellen came to me and poured out her story. It was extremely difficult for her to expose the weakness of a man she loved and whom she respected.

"We're at an impasse," she said. "There doesn't seem to be any way that Dad will ever ask forgiveness. He knows what he did. We know what he did, but he will say nothing."

We talked for a long time. We searched for options. There seemed to be none—except the one I finally suggested.

"Why don't you drive alone out to the ranch. Wait until you're sure he's by himself in the orchard and then walk up to him. When you're sure you have his full attention, then say to him, 'Dad, can you ever forgive me for what I've done?' "

"Forgive me?" Ellen cried. "Pastor, why do I need to ask his forgiveness? He's the one who's sinned, not me."

"I realize, Ellen, that your father has sinned against you—now against Tracy, but there seems to be no way that relationship can be restored.

"Why don't you try the unexpected?

"Why don't you take the initiative?

"Why don't you ask his forgiveness?"

"But what have I done?" she asked.

"Why don't you ask him to forgive you for all the anger and hate you have stored up against him for all these years?"

"I am guilty of that," she said. "It's not impossible to admit that."

We discussed the timing and the wording, and then we prayed for courage and strength. When Ellen left she was convinced that it was at least worth a try.

She called excitedly a few days later.

"It worked—it worked, Pastor, it worked."

She came over to the office and told me what had happened.

She had driven out to the ranch. When she was sure her father was in the orchard, she went in search of him. She called many times.

"Dad—Dad—Dad" until he answered. She said, "I walked over to him—filled with fear—greeted him as warmly as I could and then waited until he had finished picking up some fallen limbs.

"He finally laid them down, pulled off his gloves, and came over to where I was standing and said, 'What are you doing here?'

"I took a deep breath, swallowed as much of my nervousness as I could and then said, 'I've come to ask something of you.'

'What's that?' he said.

"I shifted nervously, wiped my palms against my dress, looked up into his face, and said, 'Dad, will you forgive me for all the anger I've had in my heart toward you for so long?' "

Henry looked with dismay into the upturned face of his anxious daughter. He struggled for words that couldn't come. He started to turn away as tears welled up in his eyes, when suddenly the high walls of silence and denial crumbled. He reached for his grown daughter, drew her to him, and began to cry unashamedly.

"Can you ever forgive me, Ellen, for what I've done to you and to Tracy?" he sobbed.

"Those were all the words that were spoken. No explanations were sought or offered, but the forgiveness was real and complete.

"Dad and I walked back to the ranch house hand

in hand. When Mom saw us, her heart leaped with fulfilled joy—but no questions were asked.

"When I was ready to leave," Ellen told me, "Dad hung on the car door for a long time before he finally asked, 'Do you think Tracy would want to help me pick some apples?'

"I sure do, Dad. When do you want us to come back?"

It took time for a little girl's fears to lessen.

It took time for a child's confidence to return.

It took time for some hideous memories to subside.

But the family is together, working through it and praying for complete freedom from their potentially destructive experience.

And Henry's reading again from his family Bible to his entire family, and they're all listening—sometimes impatiently, but they're all listening.

That's a restored relationship.

And that's the insatiable craving of us all—
  to develop a meaningful relationship
    with others,
      to understand how to keep it fresh
        and satisfying, and
          to learn how to restore it once it's
          broken.

I talked to Tracy's mother recently. It's been 18 years since these families were reconciled.

I asked her, "Is your father still living?"

"Yes," she said.

"How is your relationship with him today?"

"Wonderful," she replied. "Our relationship is wonderful."

Broken relationships can be restored, even when it involves something as sensitive and destructive as a grandfather's abuse of his granddaughter.

Fractured Friendships

Years ago I offended one of my best friends. I didn't intend to do it. In fact, I wouldn't have hurt him for the world.

Bob and I were both veterans of World War II and our families were about the same age. When Bob and his family joined the church I pastored I sensed an almost immediate affinity to him. His wife had the gift of hospitality and his mother baked delicious pies. And Bob was just plain fun to be around.

Often after a long Sunday of preaching, I would meet him in the therapeutic warmth of his outdoor pool. We talked through the day as the tiredness seeped out the pores of my body.

It wasn't long until Bob was elected to the board of the church. In his second year he became chairman. He was efficient and thorough, but occasionally he was a little brusque with people. Sometimes in discussing church-related problems he reached his bottom line far too soon.

When the congregation overextended itself in an expensive building program, funds became scarce. It was necessary to practice a frugality that many church leaders found difficult. Bob had to wear the black hat. It was his job to say "no" to the many requests for money that kept coming from various groups and individuals within the church. His answer was always the same—just one word: "Nope." He didn't explain, he didn't soften the blow, he just said, "Nope."

Bob did an excellent job of curtailing spending and eventually balancing the church budget. In the process, however, he offended some of the people. They complained to me that he was unsympathetic, uncaring, and harsh. They asked me to talk to him about it. I did.

We were in my office after a Sunday morning service making plans to get together. I said, "Bob, some of the members of the church have complained to me about your responses to their requests for church funds. Is there any way that I can be of help to you?" I had rehearsed my words many times. It was about the safest, most nonthreatening approach I could devise.

In spite of what I hoped would be a calm resolution to a sticky problem, I watched as redness spread from Bob's collar to his forehead. Then he aimed that one shattering word at me: "Nope."

Bob walked out of my office, through the church foyer, to the parking lot, and to his car. I followed him. As he opened the door of his car, I said, "Bob, I didn't mean to offend you. Can't we talk about this?"

He looked at me and repeated, "Nope." Then he climbed into his car, shut the door, and drove away.

I waited until he had time to get home and called him. His wife answered and said, "I'm sorry, but Bob is busy."

Bob was "busy" for the next 12 years. Every time I tried to reconcile the deep and complex fracture, my attempt was met with silence. We talked about church business, we made half-hearted attempts to socialize, but things were not the same. A fracture had occurred. Distance had been created. Warmth had dissipated to a horribly painful coolness.

A dozen years later I was conducting a communion service in a different church. I took a small piece of bread between my thumb and forefinger and displayed it to the worshipers. As I explained its symbolic significance, I suddenly noticed Bob sitting in the congregation. He was there—in that service—celebrating the Lord's death with me.

I could not continue.

I lowered my arm, placed the emblem of Jesus' body on the table, looked out at the people, and said,

"I'm sorry but I can't go on. There's a man here whom I offended 12 years ago and I need to ask his forgiveness."

I asked the people to bow their heads in order to protect his identity and then said to him, "Do you know who I'm talking about?" Bob nodded his head. Then I said, "My brother, will you forgive me for offending you?"

Bob sat motionless for several moments. I saw his face flush red and I feared a repeat of the fracture that had occurred 12 years earlier. Then he responded. His head went up and down. He had accepted my request.

Following the service Bob bounded down the aisle to me and said, "Don Baker, if you hadn't done that tonight, I think I would have had to. I just couldn't stand it any longer."

We hugged each other—right there in front of God and everybody. Then he said, "How about lunch on Tuesday?"

That's the insatiable craving of us all: to develop meaningful relationships with others, to understand how to keep relationships fresh and satisfying, and to learn how to restore relationships once they are broken.

Conflict is a fact of life. It can be minimized if you set up and follow ground rules for communication and relationship. It can be diminished if you accept it as inevitable. And it can be resolved by initiating biblical action. But conflict and the broken relationships it causes can never be completely avoided.

Conflict started in the perfect environment of heaven, in the very presence of God. And the one who started it there, Satan, also introduced it to earth. He has been promoting it as a way of life ever since. Satan is the author of division. He separated himself from God. He separated man from God. He separated man from woman. He separated man from man. He separated family from family and nation from nation. And eventually he separated an entire world from God.

God is the great Reconciler. In Christ, God is in the process of reconciling man to man, family to family, nation to nation, and eventually the entire world to Himself.[1]

Do you have relationships which need the Reconciler's touch? The next three chapters will give you some strategic steps you can take to put you on the road to restoration.

12

Take the Initiative

❦

Reconciliation is not optional.

Fractured relationships cannot be forgotten, ignored, or swept under the rug. They must be reconciled.

And, we must take the initiative—regardless of who's to blame.

If we are to blame, we must take the initiative. Let me repeat what Jesus says,

> If therefore you are presenting your offering at the altar, and there remember that *your brother has something against you,* leave your offering there before the altar, and go your way; first be reconciled to your brother, and then come and present your offering (Matthew 5:23,24, emphasis added).

Notice the words that suggest action:
  "leave,"
  "go," and
    "be reconciled," and then
    "come and present."

Jesus also says,

> And if your brother sins, go and reprove him in private; if he listens to you, you have won your brother (Matthew 5:15).

Again, notice the words that suggest action:
"go," and
"reprove."

If another is to blame, we still must take the initiative.

In each instance the word "go" is present.

"Go" means to take the initiative.

Ellen's experience with her father illustrates what can happen when the innocent party takes responsibility for restoring a broken relationship.

In each of Jesus' instructions for restoring broken relationships, the command to go is present and is directed to the reader. In either case to go means to take the initiative.

A Time and Place

Reconciliation is never achieved on the run. A friend waved at me after saying good-bye and said, "Hey, I'm sorry for what I said the other day." And he was gone. His apology was hardly satisfactory. That relationship was still frayed about the edges. The problem was not resolved.

Forgiveness begins in the eyes. The sincerity of both the request for forgiveness and the granting of forgiveness is seen first in the eyes. It then proceeds to the brain, filters through the heart, settles in the soul, and is finally expressed through the lips. This process requires a setting that will allow for sufficient time with no distractions, time that will permit the completion of the entire transaction.

Choose a strategic time and place for reconciliation. Select an hour of the day which will offer you a maximum amount of uninterrupted time for face-to-face conversation. Select a location which will provide at least a minimum amount of privacy. A telephone can be used if no other method is available, but a personal, one-on-one confrontation is best. I often use the phone, but I always make sure that the other person has time to talk and is free of distractions before I continue.

The setting for my apology to Bob was somewhat bizarre. Usually such a request is not made in front of hundreds in the middle of a sacred communion service. And yet isn't that what Jesus required in Matthew 5:23,24? I was in the midst of presenting my offering when I realized my urgent need to be reconciled to Bob. In that setting leaving my offering and going to Bob demanded that I act from the platform. The situation may not have been ideal, but the Holy Spirit directed the moment.

Bob's identity was kept hidden because no one was looking. Sufficient time was allowed for our brief transaction to take place. And additional time was secured later to solidify restoration and begin rebuilding the relationship.

The middle of a Monday night football game is a risky time to attempt reconciliation. I've known of some who have tried it, but then found that they had two problems to resolve. Confrontation before a meal is also risky. Low blood sugar can excite anger. Conversing in the evening while the children are still awake is often too distracting. And if you wait until you're in bed you may be too sleepy. In the morning you may be too troubled. Whenever Martha and I have a sensitive issue to discuss, we will disconnect the phone and ignore the doorbell.

Relationships are important and restoration is a necessity. Many have found that meeting for a private luncheon is a good opportunity for healing broken relationships. Couples may want to talk after a meal at home when distractions can be kept to a minimum. But even if you can't find the ideal time or place, proceed anyway. Take the risk and give the relationship the priority it deserves.

Establish Communication

Reconciliation should never be attempted until both parties are properly oriented and each one fully understands where the other is coming from. When I publicly asked for Bob's forgiveness, I alerted Bob immediately—without revealing his identity—that I was talking *about* him: "There's a man here whom I offended 12 years ago." But I wanted to be certain that he knew that I was also talking *to* him, so I asked, "Do you know who I'm talking about?" He then knew I was directing my question to him and he responded. At this point neither of us had any doubt as to what we were addressing. I had successfully established communication.

Do you remember the church leader I offended by the way I resigned? We met in my office and I initiated the conversation by asking, "Do you remember the argument we had the last time we spoke to each other?" He said he didn't. That sometimes happens. We may blow a conflict way out of proportion and remember something as being more significant than the other person does. Or he may remember something that didn't really happen to the extent he imagines.

Most often, however, we remember those hurtful events, even those which happened years ago. In our attempts to avoid further conflict we may feign forgetfulness. Sometimes we have very convenient lapses of memory. We hope that our forgetfulness will conclude the subject.

I explained just enough to the church leader to help him remember without addressing the details of the conflict. I said, "We argued over the subject of my resignation to the deacons." When he acknowledged his remembrance I knew I had established communication, and then I proceeded to seek reconciliation.

Blanket requests for forgiveness rarely cover anything. Forgiveness by indirection seldom results in reconciliation. A specific and direct reference to a specific situation is required before forgiveness can be requested.

Have you ever noticed how a little child will sometimes take your face between his little hands and force you to face him when he thinks you're not listening? That sort of physical action is hardly appropriate for adults. But sometimes, in order to affect a successful encounter for reconciliation, some attention-getting methods for establishing clear communication are necessary.

Assume Blame

Blame is usually a matter of perception. The tendency is for each person to blame the other. But in any dispute there is no innocent party. The degrees of innocence may vary. In fact, your guilt may be small compared to the offense of the other party. But any guilt, however small, can enable you to assume blame.

In my fractured relationship with Bob, I assumed blame and asked him to forgive me. What was I guilty of? What offense had I committed? For one thing my timing was wrong. After church on a Sunday morning was not a good time to discuss a problem. Remember: It's important to choose a proper time and place for confrontation. I didn't make a good choice.

More importantly, I offended Bob because he

heard me deliver a rebuke when he was just attempting to do his job. He did exactly what the board had commissioned him to do, and he did it well. The manner in which he did his job was incidental. "Nope" was his customary way to deny an irresponsible request. But instead of commending him, I made a comment which he perceived as criticism. Bob thought that his pastor and friend had deserted him at a very awkward time in the battle and had adopted the critical stance of his accusers.

The restoration of my relationship with Bob was greatly helped when I viewed my actions from his point of view. Taking Bob's perspective also enabled me to honestly assume blame.

A middle-aged woman asked me how she could reconcile her relationship with her mother who was very bitter toward her.

"What did you do?" I asked.

"Nothing," she answered. "I like my sister, but my mother dislikes her, so my mother dislikes me because I like my sister."

"Is your mother capable of saying she's sorry?" I inquired.

"I don't think so. I have never heard my mother apologize for anything."

"Then maybe you need to help her. Why don't you call her and ask her to forgive you?" I suggested.

"For what?" she asked.

"For the obvious. Ask her to forgive you for the coldness and the distance between you. Let her know that you're assuming blame for it."

"I can't do that," she insisted. "I'm not to blame."

"In her eyes you are," I answered.

She thought about it for a few days, then came back and said to me, "I sure don't want to do this unless I know the church is praying for me. They know about this and they also know it's been three years since I last talked with her."

The church prayed. The woman called her mother and returned to see me the next evening. "It worked!" she said ecstatically. "I have my mother back."

A wife unexpectedly left her husband of 20 years and their two children for the company of another man. Her husband was angry, confused, embarrassed, and lonely. As I prayed with him I was surprised to hear him say, "Father, forgive me for whatever I've done to drive my wife away. If it's my neglect or anger or indifference, please show me and forgive me."

When she did return—to stay, her requests for forgiveness were drowned out by his. Both assumed blame and both experienced healing.

Have you been waiting for someone else to take the initiative in restoring your relationship? Don't delay reconciliation any longer. Take responsibility for your relationship with this person by taking the initiative and assuming blame to start the healing process.

13

Give and Receive Forgiveness

❦

In restoring a broken relationship, choose good, safe wording.

During the communion service I said to Bob, "Will you forgive me for offending you?" I did not say, "I'm sorry for what I said" or "I want to apologize if I offended you" or any of the other "cop-out" statements which avoid the issue. The relationship was broken by an offending action, attitude, or comment. In order to heal the break, you must clarify the specific offense and ask forgiveness for it.

In my book *Love: A New Look at an Old Word*, I tell the story of the worshiper who shook my hand at the door of the church one Sunday morning and said, "Thank you, Pastor. That was a good, safe sermon."

I was baffled, confused, upset, and eventually angered by his comment. I processed those six words all Sunday afternoon and there was no way that I could find a compliment anywhere in that little sentence. If I had known the man's name I would have called him. I wanted an explanation. Did he mean that I was a compromiser? Was he telling me that I was a man-pleaser? Was he suggesting that I was afraid to address sin in my sermon? Whatever it was, he had offended me.

That Sunday night after the service I felt a presence behind me. I turned to see him waiting to talk to me. "Do you remember me, Pastor?" he asked.

I was tempted to tell him that I had been unable to forget him, but I didn't. "Yes," I answered.

"Do you remember what I said to you this morning?"

"Yes."

"I've been thinking all day about what I said," he continued. I was tempted to interrupt him and tell him what *I* had been thinking about all day, but I restrained myself. "I really didn't say what I meant to say," he said. "And when I spoke to you this morning I saw something in your eyes."

Again I was tempted to speak. I don't like people to see what's going on in my eyes. I do everything I can to hide any negative or bewildering reaction. But I let him continue.

"I sensed that I offended you," he said.

Here I wanted to argue with him by saying something like, "Offended me? You can't offend me." I wanted to convince him that I am utterly unflappable. I am not easily offended and certainly not as sensitive as he might think.

But the truth of the matter is that I am flappable, I am easily offended, and I am super-super-sensitive. I'm even sensitive about my sensitivity. Some people say sensitivity is my greatest strength. Others say it's my greatest weakness. Like it or not, strength or weakness, I am sensitive—and so are many others. I said nothing.

He went on to say, "Pastor, will you forgive me for offending you?"

I was stunned by his request. It's not that I was unfamiliar with it because I've spoken it numerous times. But the request is so seldom addressed to me. I can count on the fingers of two hands the number of times that people have asked me to forgive them. I can count on the fingers of a hundred hands the number of times I've asked forgiveness of others.

For some reason there is a rather common assumption that pastors are fair game; they're always in season and there's no limit—you can bag as many of them as you wish and as often as you please. "Since I pay my pastor's salary," we rationalize, "I can say anything about him I wish. I can criticize his dress, his sermon, his wife, his children, his automobile, his house, his speech, and his habits."

We imagine that we're covered by some sort of diplomatic immunity which keeps us from being called into account for the words or actions directed toward ministers. It's the same mentality that permitted a slave-owner to say or do anything he wished—without explanation or apology—to the man or woman he owned. And the slave had no recourse and was permitted no response.

Pastors and their wives and children bleed just like anybody else. Sometimes they bleed quicker because they're such open targets. The old adage which says "Sticks and stones may break my bones but words will never hurt me" just isn't true. Words *do* hurt. Criticisms cut. The problem is that pastors are not supposed to admit to their wounds. We're supposed to be tougher than the people in the pews. So we wear our flesh-colored Band-Aids over the nicks in our soul and pretend that nothing ever happened.

So when the man asked me to forgive him, I was stunned. But I responded right away. "Certainly I forgive you." He thanked me, and then I said, "Will you forgive me for offending you?"

He looked surprised. "What did you do to offend me?"

"You should have heard the ugly thoughts I've been thinking about you all afternoon," I replied.

He forgave me and our friendship was cemented.[1]

Have you noticed the repeated use of the words, *"Will you forgive me for offending you?"* The question is short, concise, and to the point. It leaves nothing to the imagination. It doesn't shift the blame. It requires a response. It is brief enough and safe enough to pave the way to genuine healing.

Avoid the Details

No two people remember a conversation exactly the same way. I've seen reconciliation fail as a result of an attempt to relive all the words and events that caused a fractured relationship. It's better to avoid the details and stick with the central issue of offense and forgiveness.

I have never asked my friend Bob to explain his brusque "nope" response to the requests of church leaders for funds. I have never asked him to explain his response to me when I offered my help. We have never discussed the details of those events and he has never attempted to justify his actions. Had we tried to set the details straight we would never have arrived at reconciliation because our recollection of the details would be different.

Any attempt to reach an agreement through rehearsals of an incident usually deteriorates into accusations and counter-accusations: "You said . . ."; "No, I did not say . . ."; "Yes you did, and then I said . . ."; "That's not what you said. I heard you say . . ." Attempts to unravel and explain the details often result in widening the breach between people instead of closing it. Avoid the details and concentrate on forgiveness.

Freely Give, Freely Receive

The central issue is giving and receiving forgiveness. But neither end of that transaction seems to be easy for us. Some typical responses to a request for forgiveness are: "No problem—let's just forget about it"; "You don't need my forgiveness"; "It's really no big deal"; "You didn't offend me." But all the signs in a broken relationship point in just the opposite direction of those words. The offense *cannot* be forgotten without forgiveness. The offense *needs* to be forgiven. It really *is* a big deal. And somebody really *is* offended.

"Will you forgive me for offending you?" deserves and demands a response. "Forget it" is not appropriate. The only appropriate biblical response is, "Yes, I forgive you." But for most of us, giving and receiving forgiveness is terribly difficult. We don't understand forgiveness. When someone forgives us, we feel we don't deserve it. When it's our turn to forgive someone else, we find ourselves bucking against it.

Forgiveness always seemed to be conditional when I was growing up. The usual response to any such request was met with the words, "I forgive you, but don't ever let it happen again." Well, it happened again, but I was smart enough the second time not to ask forgiveness because I was sure it wouldn't be offered. So my guilt became greater and my life phonier until I lost respect for myself completely. That's one of the ways a poor self-image develops.

Jesus' response to Peter's question is so important for us to remember: "Then Peter came and said to Him, 'Lord, how often shall my brother sin against me and I forgive him? Up to seven times?' Jesus said to him, 'I do not say to you, up to seven times, but up to seventy times seven' " (Matthew 18:21,22). A good rule of thumb is to forgive someone else at least as many times as Jesus has forgiven you.

In my book *Beyond Forgiveness*, I tell the story of an associate staff member who had a severe moral problem. He had been with me more than two years when the news reached me of his illicit affairs. When I confronted him with the information he made no attempt to deny his guilt. He had been sexually intimate with at least ten women over a period of 13 years.

The church staff and board met together to chart a course of action. The offending member was asked to:

confess to his family,
confess to the church,
resign from his position,
seek professional counseling,
refuse any invitations to public ministry, and
stay in the church until he was restored.

He agreed to all conditions.

That night I drove him home to confess to his wife. We did not speak as we traveled. There was nothing left to say. All I heard were sighs and groans from deep within his writhing soul.

When we arrived at his home it was obvious they had company. So I went to the door and asked his wife to come to the car with me. The two of them sat together in the backseat. Both were silent. She was bewildered. Finally he flung his head on her shoulder, threw his arms around her neck and said, "Can you ever forgive me? Can you ever forgive me? I've been unfaithful to you—not once but many times. Can you ever forgive me?"

I watched a scene that I'm seldom privileged to see. The color drained from the woman's face. She stiffened and withdrew, but only for a moment. She then reached her arms around her husband's shoulders and said, "Yes, I can forgive you."

What kind of woman is this? I wondered when I heard her response. It was not the response I expected. It was not the usual response from a betrayed wife. When I was writing *Beyond Forgiveness* some time later I asked her about her response. "Did you really mean that?"

"Yes," she answered.

"How could you respond so positively to your husband's confession?"

"I grew up on forgiveness," she replied. "One of the first lessons we learned as children was the lesson of forgiveness. My parents forgave us. They taught us to forgive each other. They modeled forgiveness in front of us. We memorized and sang Ephesians 4:32: 'Be kind to one another, tender-hearted, forgiving each other, just as God in Christ also has forgiven you.' "

"Didn't you struggle at all with your forgiveness of him?" I asked.

"Oh yes," she said. "I had my times of anger and bitterness. Our reconciliation required sessions with his counselor, and I wondered at times if things would ever be right with us again. But I did forgive him."

"How did you convince him that you had forgiven him?" I asked.

"There were a number of things I did," she said.

"I told him that I forgave him.

And that I loved him.

I stayed with him,

I cooked his meals,

I washed his clothes,

I packed his lunches,

I slept with him, and

I initiated sex with him."

"You did what?" I asked, dumbfounded.

"I initiated sex with him."

"That's profound," I said. "Do you mind if I include that in the book?"

"Not at all," she answered. "That's what forgiveness is all about."

Today this couple is back in the ministry—fully restored to God, to each other, and to their church family. They are both enjoying the marriage they always wanted. Their relationship is a living tribute to the power of forgiveness.[2]

A young college woman asked me how she could free herself from the bitterness she felt against her divorced parents.

"Ask their forgiveness," I replied.

"For what? They're the ones who sinned against me. I'm the one who should be doing the forgiving."

"Ask them to forgive you for the obvious: your anger toward them."

"That won't make me feel any better," she complained.

"It might," I answered. "But feeling better isn't the only thing you want to achieve. You want a relationship restored."

She did ask her parents to forgive her. She did the thing they least expected and she received in return the thing she least expected: a restored relationship. She joined the chorus of others who have returned to me saying, "It works!"

Giving and receiving forgiveness is the central issue in restoring relationships.

Giving and receiving forgiveness liberates both the offender and the offended.

Giving and receiving forgiveness is the divine weapon that completely disarms a hostile and guilty world.

Forgiveness is God's way of restoring relationships—and it's not optional. We are commanded to seek reconciliation and to give and receive forgiveness.

Have you been dodging the central issue in your fractured relationships? Have you skirted the importance of giving and receiving forgiveness? Get right to the heart of the matter. It will work for you too.

14

Reestablish the Relationship

❦

Bob's invitation for me to join him for lunch on Tuesday was the final step in the restoration of our relationship. It's one thing to resolve a problem; it's quite another to reconcile a relationship. The previous two steps—taking the initiative and giving and receiving forgiveness—are designed to resolve a problem. Once problems are resolved, people must be reconciled.

The problem of sin was resolved between Jesus and Zaccheus when Jesus saw him in the sycamore tree and ordered him to come down. But the healing of their relationship began when Jesus went home with him (Luke 19:1-10).

After forgiveness has been given and received, move right back into the pre-problem relationship as far as you can go. You might do so by extending an invitation to dinner, to coffee, to play golf, or to go shopping. Reconciliation may include returning to a discussion of business concerns which is typical of your earlier relationship. In the case of my staff member who experienced moral failure, his wife reinitiated family life and sexual activity with him. As she said, returning the relationship to its former level is what forgiveness is all about.

You might also want to joyfully share the experience of your reconciliation with someone who has faithfully prayed for you—just like you shared your conversion experience with others.

Rebuilding Takes Time

In attempting to reestablish a relationship, don't expect too much too soon. Paul tells us in Philippians 3:13 to forget what lies behind. For some people that's extremely difficult. Some of us can't remember anything except the wrongs that have been committed against us. The human tendency is to remember the negative and forget the positive. Memory can be a helpful tool for resisting the same temptation again. But memory, when we allow it to punish us, is a destructive weapon.

Give people time when complete restoration comes slower than you think it should. Allow time for them to prove their good intentions and change their style of living. Allow time for your wounds to heal and for your system to shake off the shock of disillusionment. God doesn't need time, but we often do.

Time is also necessary for working through the "what ifs" of rebuilding a relationship. You may ask, "What if he says he forgives me but continues to tell others what I've done?" This is the ultimate insult to the concept of forgiveness.

Some people have extended forgiveness to me and then used my request for forgiveness to justify themselves and destroy me in the eyes of others. "See," they say, "he even admitted he was wrong." My admission is interpreted as a sign of weakness or failure rather than a mark of strength. This response comes from people like the man who boasted to me, "I have never sinned, I have never cried, and I have never said I'm sorry." What a pitiful commentary on a totally empty life. What a travesty of the truth. What an admission of weakness. What a way to permanently destroy a relationship.

You may ask, "What if he doesn't really mean it when he says he is sorry for offending me?" Some don't. The genuineness of repentance is something known only to God; however, it can usually be trusted if the guilty party is willing to become accountable to you.

True repentance submits to accountability. If an individual is willing to accept whatever restrictions or disciplines are imposed on him, we can be reasonably sure of the genuineness of his repentance. That's one of the reasons my former staff member, who was disciplined for moral failure, is in the ministry today. His repentance was sincere, as attested to by his willingness to submit to the plan for his restoration determined by our church leaders.

Forgiveness is a grace gift from God. It's His nature to forgive. It's not my nature, however, and probably not yours either. But forgiveness is essential to the process of healing a broken relationship even when sincerity is in doubt.

When Death Interrupts

In some cases a broken relationship cannot be reestablished because the other person has died. Perhaps you intended to restore a relationship with a parent, child, or friend, but a sudden fatal illness or injury took them from you before forgiveness could be given or received.

A young man came to talk to me about his abusive father and the anger and bitterness which had plagued him since childhood. "How can I be free from this anger toward my father?" he asked.

"Ask his forgiveness," I replied.

"But my father is dead."

"Is he buried near the community?"

"Yes."

"Have you ever thought of spending time at his grave venting all the hostility you feel? Tell him what you're thinking and ask him to forgive you," I suggested.

It was a new thought to him and he resisted it at first. Finally he said, "I'll try anything. I'll even go to the cemetery and talk to a dead man if it will relieve me of this burden I've been carrying."

Three times he visited his father's grave and verbalized his deep, painful feelings. After each visit he came up to me at church and expressed some limited relief. After he visited his father's grave for the fourth time he came to see me after the Sunday evening service. He waited until everyone else had gone, then came to me and thanked me. With tear-filled eyes he said, "This afternoon I was finally able to tell my dad I loved him."

If for some reason you are unable to reestablish a broken relationship due to death, separation, or hostility in the other person, you may need to realize your healing in an indirect manner as this young man did.

Many mothers have asked me how they can experience the forgiveness of the unborn child they aborted. Let me share a story from my book *Beyond Choice* about how one young mother was finally relieved of the painful guilt she suffered after three abortions.

Debbie could not receive forgiveness from the babies she had aborted, nor could she forgive herself. A wise counselor led her out of her pain. He began by asking, "How do you feel about the unborn babies you aborted?"

"Terrible, guilty, sad, angry. I've often wished there was some way I could tell them how sorry I am."

She began to weep. "If I could only talk to them and ask them to forgive me. Everyone I've asked has said that they were not really human beings, but somehow I can't believe that. I feel little eyes staring at me and pleading with me to tell the doctors to stop. I didn't stop. I just let them do it. I let them kill my little babies."

"Would you like to talk to one of those babies, Debbie?" the counselor asked.

"Oh yes, if only I could. I can't sleep at night. I feel so condemned for what I've done."

The counselor got up from behind his desk, walked around to the center of the room, and placed two empty chairs there facing each other. He asked Debbie to sit in one of the empty chairs, then he seated himself behind her out of her range of vision.

"Debbie," he said, "I want you to forget that I'm in the room with you. For a little while I'm going to be completely silent. I want you to imagine that the empty chair in front of you is your little baby, the baby you aborted in the Columbia River Medical Clinic. How old was that fetus?"

"Just 12 weeks," she answered.

"How was it aborted?"

"By suction."

"How did you feel when it was happening?"

"I just kept asking it to forgive me. All the time that tube was inside me tearing that little baby out of me, I kept telling it how sorry I was, that I couldn't help it, that they were making me do it."

"Why don't you talk to your baby now. Just pretend that the chair is your baby. Forget that I'm here. Tell the baby what you think it wants to hear."

Debbie looked at the empty chair for a long time. It was hard for her to visualize anything but a chair in front of her. But the longer she looked at it and thought about it, the more she sensed something happening deep inside her. She felt pain, sorrow, and anguish. An emptiness gripped her and tore at her until her whole body began to convulse with sobs.

She slid down to the floor and knelt in front of the empty chair, burying her head in its cushion. "Oh my baby, my baby," she cried. "I'm so sorry. Please forgive me. I didn't mean to do it. I didn't want to do it. I wouldn't have hurt you for anything in the world. All I wanted to do was to hold you and to nurse you and to change you and to feed you. I wanted to love you. Tim wanted to love you. We both wanted to love you together. You were our baby. You were the result of our love and we wanted to keep you, but they wouldn't let us.

"I miss you so much. At nights I can hear you crying for me. I get up to get a bottle and find that you're only a dream. I wanted to feel your little head on my arm, on my breast, against my cheek. I wanted to buy you little clothes and wrap you in little blankets. I wanted to look at you while you were sleeping and watch you when you were awake.

"I wanted to help you take your first step and listen to you speak your first word. I wanted to buy your first shoes and fix your meals. I wanted to watch you leave for your first day at school and then have you come home and tell me all about it. I wanted you and I still want you."

Suddenly Debbie groaned and wailed as if the intense pain was more than she could bear. Then she screamed, "I'm sorry, I'm sorry. Please, please forgive me."

She lay on the floor in an exhausted heap. She was completely spent, finally emptied of an emotion that she had been suppressing for years.

The wise and compassionate counselor reached down and lifted Debbie to her feet, wrapped his arms around her, and held her tight until her sobbing stopped. Debbie had finally experienced healing from her broken relationships with her babies.[1]

Are you actively seeking to reestablish relationships with someone you have forgiven or with someone who has forgiven you? If not, when will you begin? Did you have a broken relationship with someone which was never reconciled because of his or her death? Healing is available to you.

PART IV

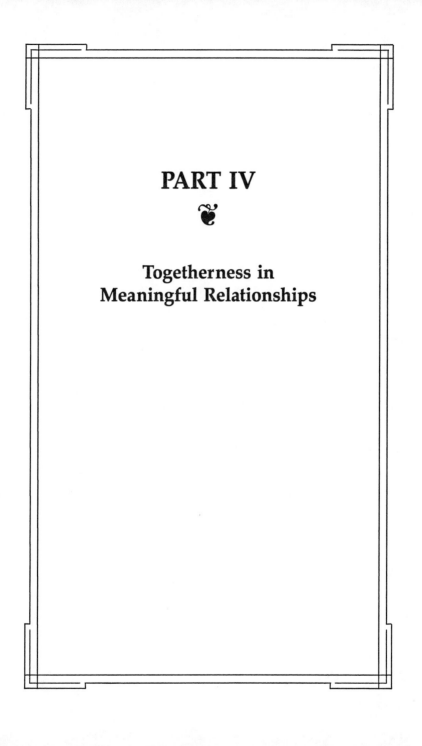

Togetherness in Meaningful Relationships

15

Growing Meaningful Relationships through Groups

❧

It is possible for almost everyone to experience a meaningful relationship. But some people resist oneness with others because meaningful relationships require self-disclosure and self-discipline. Many others resist because they are afraid that intimate involvement with others will lead to rejection.

I harbored some of those same feelings. But my experience of recovery from deep depression through the ministry of Emery Nester and others taught me the value of close personal relationships. When Emery gave me 100 hours of counseling he did far more listening than he did talking. He allowed me the fulfillment of a wish: to filter all my thoughts, experiences, and ideas through the mind of another person in a nonthreatening environment. It was a profound, life-changing experience for me. Through my interaction with Emery I found that I was human after all, that what I felt and did was common to everyone, that my problems were the same problems everyone faced, and that the solutions I needed had been discovered by others and could be applied to my situation.

I grew personally through my relationship with Emery Nester as I had never grown before. It's the kind of deep committed relationship in which everyone can grow. But convincing others of the value of the process is still extremely difficult. Many of us grew up in legalistic churches and were taught to live by rules and regulations which we found very difficult to keep. Rather than admit our failures, we hid them from others and tried to hide them from ourselves.

What we don't realize is that everyone else is trying to hide their failures also. Growth comes when we finally find that safe place in meaningful relationships where we can admit the truth and still be loved. James said: "Confess your sins to one another, and pray for one another, so that you may be healed" (James 5:16). This concept is not only theologically significant, it is also psychologically profound. Not everyone will feel free to reveal their weaknesses and failures to others, but for those who do the experience becomes life-changing. It can even change a church.

Grouping for Growth

Over 200 years ago John Wesley introduced his solution to the loneliness and alienation that existed among Christians in his day. He gathered his people together in small groups called Methodist "societies." These societies became the secret strength of Methodism.

Wesley's small groups were not designed to be instructional sessions. They were for fellowship, a time for the members of a large congregation to get to know each other in small, conversation-sized groups. They talked about the inner life, their failures, their victories, and their Lord. The Methodist societies were so successful that, several years ago, a prominent Congregational minister remarked to G. Campbell Morgan, "You know, Morgan, if I could do it, I would graft the Methodist class meeting into the Congregational system, and I would make attendance at it obligatory to membership."

In the last 40 years there has been increasing interest in small groups. Big churches, busy communities, increased loss of personal identity, and society's every-increasing mobility have turned us back toward each other in search of more meaningful relationships.

Small groups came into prominence again in the 1950s. Campus Crusade, The Navigators, Yokefellows, Faith at Work, and Bible Study Fellowship began promoting them as growth experiences—but only outside the parameters of the local church. Their focus was primarily Bible study.

In the '60s the small group movement continued largely as a parachurch ministry encouraged by men like Keith Miller and Bruce Larson. The focus of many of the small group ministries arising in this decade was community action.

In the '70s small groups in the Christian community were strongly influenced by secular encounter groups. The focus was on personal growth—psychological as well as spiritual.

In the '80s small groups were widely accepted by Christians. They were integrated into the church as an implement of meaningful individual and corporate growth. Small groups came of age as an essential ministry for helping individuals find a meaningful balance in their lives. Roberta Hestenes helped clarify the ministry of a small group by identifying it as "an intentional face-to-face gathering of three to twelve people on a regular time schedule with a common purpose of discovering and growing in the possibilities of the abundant life in Christ."[1]

In Seoul, Korea, Pastor Paul Yonggi Cho attempted to build a church in the traditional manner until it completely sapped him of his strength. In 1961 the Holy Spirit impressed upon him the idea of starting home cell groups as the basis for spiritual life and fellowship in the congregation. When Cho's small group ministry began, the church numbered only a few hundred. By 1988 the church had grown to 250,000 members, largely through the ministry of the home cell groups which meet throughout the city.

In the early 1950s the doors of ministry to China closed and foreign missionaries were expelled. Chinese Christians numbered approximately one million at the time. Suffering persecution for their public expressions of faith, believers moved from church buildings to secret house churches. These "cottage meetings" focused on fellowship and nurture. Today conservative estimates number the Christian community in China at 50 million believers, largely the result of the impact of the small house churches.

The 90s have already been dubbed by some the decade of relationships. The tide of small group popularity and effectiveness is projected to surge even higher.

The Small Group Advantage

Small groups include some of the same features found in large congregations: worship, discipling, and evangelism for example. But small groups facilitate the spirit of oneness like few congregations can. It is in the small group that relationships can develop. It is there that walls between people are broken down. It is there that the unity of the Spirit can develop and spread to other Christians.

In his book *The Problem of Wineskins*, Howard Snyder lists a number of advantages of the small group ministry within the church: "It is flexible—it can change. It is mobile—it can move. It is inclusive—it is open. It is personal—it meets *my* needs. It is risky—vulnerability grows. It is evangelistic—it attracts others."[2]

As one church that I pastored grew, the need for small groups became critical. Joel MacDonald joined our staff and assumed the responsibility for supervising a small group ministry. Churches Alive, under the leadership of Howard Ball, entered into a consulting relationship with us. Ron Wormser, formerly of Campus Crusade for Christ, assumed the role of our consultant for small group ministry.

Our primary thrust at the outset was to develop leaders. We selected people who showed potential for leadership and each person or couple was asked to make a 19-24 month commitment.

Then we started with four groups of 12-14 persons each with singles and marrieds included in all groups. We stressed four areas of concern in each small group meeting.

First, we learned to share truth. A prescribed Bible study with opportunity for interaction was included in the meeting plan.

Second, we learned to share needs. Intimacy and oneness developed in our groups as people progressively shared more personal needs. It took time for people to feel comfortable to share their needs. In some groups it took months. But it eventually happened.

Third, we learned to share prayer. We shared requests and answers. Trust in one another developed as we opened our hearts to each other. Trust in God grew as He opened His heart to us.

Fourth, we learned to share Christ. Each small group member prepared a one-minute testimony, memorized Scriptures for witnessing, and learned some basic tools for making Christ known to others.

Did small groups work for us? Yes and no. On the plus side, a tremendous bonding between members took place in the small group structure. Many emotional, spiritual, and personal needs of individual church members were met in the small groups. The workload of the pastoral staff was eased as lay members began ministering to each other. Couples and singles found their lives changed. Retired couples found themselves memorizing Scripture together for the first time in their lives. Leaders were trained in our small groups. Some of them went on to lead other groups and others assumed leadership roles in the church.

On the minus side, the process of equipping leaders and forming groups, although thorough, was too slow. It took 18 months to train a group leader, which meant that the number of groups could not increase as rapidly as we hoped they would. But we kept developing leaders and forming groups until about 1,500 of our people were involved in the small group ministry.

Oneness Through Small Groups

Lyman Coleman, a pioneer and leader in the small group movement, has identified at least 15 different kinds of small group structures, each with a slightly different focus or methodology. Despite the wide variety of forms, the general feeling of those involved in these ministries is that small groups are doing what they were created to do: provide a structure for developing relationships where people feel accepted and cared for.

Dr. Cho describes his church in Korea as the smallest church in the world as well as the biggest church in the world. Every member is part of a cell group consisting of no more than 15 families. Each week church members meet in their neighborhood cell groups to worship, to pray, to learn from the Scriptures, to experience the ministry and the gifts of the Holy Spirit, and to enjoy loving relationships with fellow Christians.

In a congregation of 250,000, it's easy for individuals to be seen as numbers instead of names. On Sunday they meet in shifts for a very traditional service in one of the largest auditoriums in the world. But in Cho's home cell groups everyone is known by name and cared for as an individual. Cell groups have the opportunity to do what cannot be done in the larger congregational meetings. Group members can minister to one another with the spiritual gifts that have been given to them.

In China the cell group was God's survival tactic for the persecuted church. Christians met secretly in small groups to worship and share Scriptures which they had committed to memory since all Bibles had been confiscated. They shared testimonies about God's faithfulness and prayed together.

These groups of committed, caring Christians in China and Korea emitted an irresistibly attractive fragrance of love. Lonely, alienated people were drawn into these groups, and thousands have come to know Jesus Christ as Savior.

Em Griffin says that all good groups seem to have at least three things in common.

First, they are cohesive. A group identity and loyalty develops that enables them to stick together and stay together.

Second, they are inclusive. Effective groups absorb any and all who want to be involved regardless of the traits which tend to divide people.

Third, they are committed. Their commitment might be to a cause, to a period of time, or to the accomplishment of a specific goal. They may simply commit themselves to meet together until they have attained a spirit of oneness and peace.[4]

Small groups, regardless of structure or size, are essential to the development of meaningful relationships. It's in the small group that we come to accept and even appreciate our differences as individuals. If you are going to love, encourage, and serve Christ with a group of believers, you must get to know them and they must get to know you. Meaningful relationships like these can only happen in groups designed for and committed to that purpose.

Are you presently being nurtured in a small group of believers who mutually accept and care for each other? Are you seeking to build meaningful relationships through your committed involvement with others?

16

The Leaders of Small Group Ministry

❦

Selecting the right leaders for small group ministry is essential. Effective training will help recruited leaders develop some of the practical skills for leading small groups. But there are some basic qualities which should be present in those who are to be equipped for leadership in this vital ministry. Here are ten traits which should be evident in some measure in prospective small group leaders:

1. *Leaders should be people of the Spirit.* In the spiritual ministry of helping people develop meaningful small group relationships, it is essential that leaders understand the person and work of the Holy Spirit. It is God's Spirit who breaks down the barriers which separate people. He molds people together into caring groups. Oneness is the Spirit's domain and it can never be accomplished by leaders whose dependence is on the flesh.

2. *Leaders should be people of the Word.* Small group ministry does not require spiritual or theological giants or biblical experts. But since the foundation for meaningful relationships is found in God's Word, group leaders should have an insatiable hunger for truth and an unquestioning willingness to obey it.

3. *Leaders should be people of prayer.* Since prayer plays such a vital role in leading us to experience the unity of the Spirit, group leaders must know how to pray. I'm not talking about people who have mastered the correct form, style, or words of prayer. I'm talking about people whose lives are punctuated by the reality of daily experiences in prayer. Leaders should know and be able to share the valid significance of specific prayer, praise, and confession.

4. *Leaders should be people who like people.* Some people don't like people. Some people relate better to ideas and concepts. Some people are more at home dealing with inanimate physical objects, paperwork, or details. Some people are just hermits. The only people who truly qualify to lead small groups are people who like to be with people.

5. *Leaders should be people who are committed to people.* It is important that small group leaders are willing to commit themselves to influence, to participate with, and to become change agents in the lives of others. The people-commitment demands are so great in this ministry that small group leaders should have no other responsibilities in their church.

6. *Leaders should be people who know pain.* Since small group leaders will be involved with people who are struggling with a wide range of spiritual, emotional, relational, and physical problems, they will be at an advantage if they have grown through similar painful experiences. Compassion is essential to those who want to help people develop relationships. And compassion only grows in a climate of suffering.

7. *Leaders should be people who know how to listen.* Human communication goes far beyond what the

tongue speaks and the ear hears. People often say things which are far different from what they are really thinking or feeling. Good leaders are able and willing to listen until they hear what the speaker really means, whether or not it's what he says.

8. *Leaders should be people who know how to ask questions.* Have you noticed that many members of a group are reticent to make contributions to the discussion? They are just waiting for someone to ask them what they think or how they feel. Questions are essential for drawing out the hidden, untapped wealth of a group's knowledge, opinions, and experiences. Being a good questioner also requires the discipline of letting others speak instead of monopolizing the discussion.

9. *Leaders should be people who are vulnerable.* Do you remember the meaning of vulnerability? A vulnerable person is one who is willing to risk injury for the sake of another. The statement "I know what you mean because I struggle with that problem too" can often go a long way to opening a group to frankness and honesty with each other.

10. *Leaders should be people who are willing to struggle.* Oneness can often only be achieved through disagreement and conflict. A leader must be willing to allow differences and disagreements to emerge. Conflict must be verbalized, explored, and understood. Leaders must be ready to struggle through the process when people and their ideas and feelings clash. Oneness can never be experienced where conflict is suppressed.

You may be discouraged with the above list because you think people with these qualities are rare. True, there are not many people who immediately qualify. But that's where God's Spirit and God's grace come into play. The Holy Spirit is the author and source of these qualities. He can take people who are in the process of developing these traits and miraculously mature them and use them at the same time. Without the Spirit's equipping, no one can lead.

Small groups may need periodic changes of leadership and direction. They may even need to be terminated. The life span of a small group ministry is unpredictable. It will vary with the changing personality and needs of the congregation. But the meaningful relationships these groups produce will be permanent.

Are the qualities of a small group leader developing in your life? Are you exercising these qualities to help build oneness in your relationships?

17

Preserve Oneness at All Costs

❧

Relationships, whether with individuals or in groups, require constant attention and care.

I was walking into one of Portland's large hospitals when I heard a crisp announcement over the building's loudspeaker that said, "All automobiles parked in the fire lanes are to be moved immediately."

There was no explanation—not even a "please."

I walked back outside and became aware of the curbs, painted red and marked with the words "Fire Zone," that completely circled the complex of buildings.

As I studied the fire zones, I was struck with the thought that someone here must think that something in these buildings is valuable enough to deserve very thorough protection.

The apostle Paul inserts a fire zone right in the midst of his famous church growth passage in Ephesians 4.

He begins with an exhortation to us as individuals:

> I . . . entreat you to walk in a manner worthy of the calling with which you have been called, with all humility and gentleness, with patience, showing forbearance to one another in love (Ephesians 4:1,2).

Then comes the fire zone:
> Being diligent to preserve the unity of the
> Spirit in the bond of peace (Ephesians
> 4:3).

The apostle must think that Christian relationships are valuable enough to deserve very thorough protection.

The unity of the Spirit, or oneness, is a prized possession—of infinite value—to be protected and preserved at all costs.

When it was first achieved in Jerusalem, it resulted in the unleashing of such Holy Spirit power that the entire city was shaken for God. Nations had their representative converts. The world suddenly became Christ-conscious.

The first crisis to threaten oneness was economic. There were "haves" and "have-nots."

The "haves" shared with the "have-nots," and the crisis passed (Acts 2:45; 4:34,35).

The second crisis to threaten oneness was political. Peter and John were put into prison (Acts 4:3). Upon their release they called the believers together and they prayed. They asked God for boldness. God answered and supplied exactly what they had requested (Acts 4:23-31).

The third crisis to threaten oneness was rivalry.

Ananias and Sapphira wanted some of the recognition that had been given to Barnabas for his unselfish contributions to the poor. They sold their property, gave the money earned from it to the apostles and suggested they were giving all.

God slew them—both.

The fourth crisis to threaten oneness was jealousy.

The high priest and all his associates were filled with it (Acts 5:17) and put the apostles in a public jail.

During the night, the angel of the Lord opened the gates and set them free (Acts 5:19).

The fifth crisis to threaten oneness was complaining.

The Hellenistic Jews felt they were being slighted in the distribution of food.

The apostles interrupted their high task of world evangelization in favor of oneness and established an organization called "Deacons" to take care of feeding the widows.

The sixth crisis to threaten oneness was death. Stephen, in the midst of providing a powerful message, was stoned.

Jesus, in heaven, rose from His place of honor at His Father's right hand to encourage the dying martyr and then later sent a bolt of lightning down upon Stephen's persecutor, Saul of Tarsus, and converted him.

Oneness encircled the heretical Samaritans in Acts 8 and reached out further to encircle the pagan Gentiles in chapter 10.

Oneness is again threatened in Acts 15, when a doctrinal dispute arose regarding the subject of salvation.

Again, world evangelization came to a halt. Paul and Barnabas were recalled from their missionary journeys; the apostles assembled and spent the necessary time clarifying the doctrine and preserving oneness (Acts 15:1-35).

And then oneness was fractured:

> Barnabas was desirous of taking John, called Mark, along with them also. But Paul kept insisting that they should not take him along who had deserted them in Pamphylia and had not gone with them to the work. And there arose such a sharp

> disagreement that they separated from one another, and Barnabas took Mark with him and sailed away to Cyprus (Acts 15:37-39).

The giants of the faith squabbled.

And it wasn't even a theological dispute. It was something far less significant than the great doctrinal debate in the same chapter. It was an argument over whether or not Mark was worthy to accompany them.

It's encouraging to me to see that even Paul and Barnabas had feet of clay. I'm glad I'm not the only one who squabbles and separates from people over lesser issues.

But they reconciled. They healed their fractured relationship. They didn't stubbornly insist that their decision had been right.

They were reconciled.

Paul commended Mark for his usefulness in the last letter he wrote (2 Timothy 4:11).

Throughout his writings, Paul interrupts his doctrinal and practical exhortations to appeal for oneness.

To the Romans he said,

> Now may the God who gives perseverance and encouragement grant you to be of the *same* mind with *one another* according to Christ Jesus; that with *one* accord you may with *one* voice glorify the God and Father of our Lord Jesus Christ (Romans 15:5,6, emphasis added).

To the Corinthians he said,

> Now I exhort you, brethren, by the name of our Lord Jesus Christ, that you *all* agree, and that there be *no divisions* among you, but you be made complete in the *same*

mind and in the *same* judgment (1 Corinthians 1:10, emphasis added).

To the Ephesians he said,
Preserve the *unity* of the Spirit (Ephesians
4:3, emphasis added).

To the Philippians he said,
Make my joy complete by being of the
same mind, maintaining the *same* love,
united in spirit, intent on *one* purpose
(Philippians 2:2, emphasis added).

To the Colossians he said,
Bearing with *one another*, and forgiving
each other, whoever has a complaint against
any one; just as the Lord forgave you, so
also should you (Colossians 3:13, emphasis
added).

To Timothy he interrupted his remarks to remind
them of those who would disrupt with
disputes about words, and
envy, and
strife, and
abusive language, and
suspicions.
(1 Timothy 6:4).

Oneness is prized and valuable. Without it the
body of Christ is powerless.

It needs the protection of a fire zone that rings
our relationships completely and keeps them intact.

Our role as a peacemaker never ends.

We must be constantly on guard to protect the
body from that which would divide it.

But let me warn you: Peacemaking is a costly and
hazardous profession. It sometimes costs more to
keep the peace than it does to win the war.

Peacemaking cost God His Son.

It cost Jesus His life.

It will cost us the price of eternal vigilance and sleepless nights and prayerful agony and sometimes the frightening intervention.

The most stressful responsibility of Christians today is that of "preserving the unity of the Spirit in the bond of peace."

But the spiritual unity we preserve and defend is the sharpest evangelistic tool we have at our disposal and the most irresistible attraction we have to offer a
> fractured,
>> alienated, and
>>> lonely world.

It's time now—time to add a new priority—one that's as old as the Gospel.

It's time to stop fighting and start loving.

It's time to stress relationships.

It's time to preach unity.

It's time to emphasize oneness.

It's time to lift the church out of its isolation and alienation and elevate it to its place of original intention.

It's time to model oneness in Christian marriage and Christian families.

It's time to show the world that Jesus came not only to provide eternal life, but to change the quality of life in time. He came to provide the means by which 2, 10, 100, or 1000 people and more can dispel their loneliness and enjoy meaningful relationships forever.

Notes

Chapter 1
1. Christopher Anderson, *People*, August 22, 1977, p. 30.
2. Maya Pines, "Psychological Hardness: The Role of Challenge in Health," *Psychology Today*, December, 1980, p. 43.
3. *People*, February 15, 1989, p. 61.

Chapter 4
1. M. Scott Peck *The Different Drum* (Simon and Schuster, 1987), adapted from pp. 13-14.
2. Keith Miller, *The Scent of Love*, pp. 205-206.

Chapter 5
1. C. Norman Krause, *The Community of the Spirit* (William B. Eerdmans Publishing Co., 1974), adapted from pp. 12-13.
2. *Ryrie Study Bible* (Moody Press, 1976), p. 1448.
3. Krause, *Community of the Spirit*, p. 23.

Chapter 6
1. Quoted in Gerard Norenberg, *How to Read a Person Like a Book* (Pocket Books, 1975).

Chapter 7
1. V. Gilbert Beers, *Parents, Talk with Your Children* (Harvest House Publishers, 1988), p. 15.

Chapter 8
1. David Seamands, *Healing for Damaged Emotions* (Victor Books, 1981).

Chapter 11
1. Adapted from Don Baker, *Acceptance* (Multnomah Press, 1985).

Chapter 13
1. Adapted from Don Baker, *Love: A New Look at an Old Word* (Harvest House Publishers, 1988).
2. Adapted from Don Baker, *Beyond Forgiveness* (Multnomah Press, 1985).

Chapter 14
1. Adapted from Don Baker, *Beyond Choice* (Multnomah Press).

Chapter 15
1. Lyman Coleman, *Serendipity Training Manual for Groups* (Serendipity House, 1987).
2. Howard Snyder, *The Problem of Wineskins* (Inter-Varsity Press, 1975).

Other Good Harvest House Reading

INTIMACY
The Longing of Every Human Heart
by *Terry Hershey*

Terry explains why we often simultaneously crave *and* fear intimacy, and how that draws us toward successive patterns of hurt and frustration—in friendships, dating, and marriage. More importantly, he tells us how we can experience balanced, healthy human relationships—by *first* establishing an intimate relationship with our Heavenly Father.

IN GOD'S WORD
Devotional Studies to Enrich Your Life with God's Truth
by *Nancie Carmichael*

With a firm belief that the Bible is meant to be a personal "handbook" for living, Nancie Carmichael began her *personal* Bible study years ago as a young pastor's wife. Today she is the copublisher of *Virtue* magazine along with her husband, Bill, and leads their over 130,000 subscribers in a Bible study each month. *In God's Word* is the compilation of the years of diligent effort and care Nancie has brought to the Bible study column of *Virtue*. Embark on a great *personal* adventure as you get to know the Lord more intimately through daily time in His Word.

THE CHURCH IS NOT FOR PERFECT PEOPLE
by *William J. Murray*

New Christians versus lifelong Christians—can the struggles of understanding and relating to each other be overcome in the church? William J. Murray, son of Madalyn Murray O'Hair and author of the bestseller

My Life Without God, reveals the kinds of problems he and many new Christians face as they try to fit into the modern church. *The Church Is Not for Perfect People* covers topics such as learning the language and clichés of the Christian church; facing marital discord when one spouse does not receive Christ; the struggle of singles—especially divorced singles—who try to fit into a church geared to couples; and the lack of church support for new Christians who need help dealing with past problems such as alcohol, drug abuse, and sexual temptations. *The Church Is Not for Perfect People* takes a much-needed and realistic look at how the church can be supportive of Christians who are emerging from a humanistic society.

CLASSIC CHRISTIANITY
Life's too short to miss out on the real thing!
by *Bob George*

In this remarkable book, Bob George shares in his down-to-earth style the road back to joy and contentment in the Christian life. Drawing on his years of teaching and counseling experience, Bob clearly outlines the common pitfalls and misconceptions that are hindering so many Christians today and robbing them of the experience of their inheritance in Christ. He confronts the question of why so many Christians start out as enthusiastic believers and then decide that Christianity doesn't "work" for them. He then provides the truth that will help Christians get back on track and stay there.

Bob George, founder and president of Discipleship Counseling Services, is the counselor and teacher on "People to People," a daily biblical counseling program broadcast live via satellite on radio stations from coast to coast. Bob has authored numerous Bible study books and curricula for training men and women in personal ministry.